RAILWAYS OF LINCOLNSHIRE

PAUL ANDERSON

Lincolnshire is largely rural and so were its railways. The paraphernalia of a country branch line nearing its market town terminus is beautifully portrayed in this study of the approach to Stamford East on 31st May 1958. The tiny engine shed and Great Northern signal box were delightful enough, but the terminus itself was one of the most exquisite stations in the country. Photograph R.C. Riley.

IRWELL PRESS

Ex-Great Central class N5 0-6-2 tank No.69258 leaving Stamford Town with a freight on 24th June 1958. Photograph R.C. Riley.

**Published by
IRWELL PRESS
15 Lovers Lane, Grasscoft, Oldham OL4 4DP
Printed by Amadeus Press
Huddersfield**

CONTENTS

NOTE:- On maps in the text, existing railways are shown as continuous lines and closed railways as dotted lines. Stations retaining passenger services are shown as solid circles and closed stations as open circles.

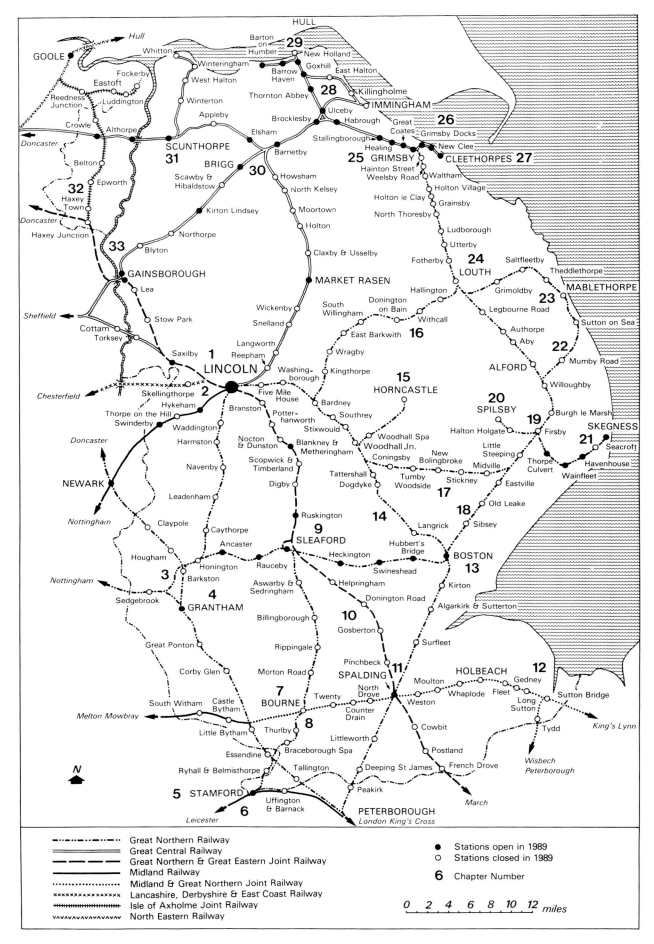

HULL

GOOLE
Hull →

Whitton
Winteringham
West Halton
Winterton
Appleby
Elsham
Barnetby

Fockerby
Eastoft
Reedness Junction
Luddington
Crowle
Althorpe
Belton
Epworth
SCUNTHORPE 31
BRIGG 30

Barton on Humber **29**
New Holland
Barrow Haven
Goxhill
East Halton
Killingholme
IMMINGHAM 26
Thornton Abbey **28**
Brocklesby
Ulceby
Habrough
Great Coates
Grimsby Docks
Stallingborough
Healing
New Clee
Grimsby Docks **26**
GRIMSBY 25
CLEETHORPES 27

Haxey Town **32**
Haxey Junction **33**
Blyton
Northorpe
Kirton Lindsey
Scawby & Hibaldstow
Howsham
North Kelsey
Moortown
Holton
Claxby & Usselby
MARKET RASEN
Wickenby
Snelland
Langworth
Reepham

Hainton Street
Weelsby Road
Waltham
Holton Village
Holton le Clay
Grainsby
North Thoresby
Ludborough
Utterby
Fotherby
LOUTH 24
Saltfleetby
Theddlethorpe
MABLETHORPE
Grimoldby
Legbourne Road
Sutton on Sea
Authorpe
Aby **22**
Mumby Road
ALFORD
Willoughby
Hallington
Donington on Bain
Withcall **16**
South Willingham
East Barkwith
Wragby
Kingthorpe

GAINSBOROUGH
Lea
Stow Park
Cottam
Torksey
Saxilby **1**
LINCOLN
Washingborough
Five Mile House
Bardney
Southrey
Stixwould
Woodhall Spa
Woodhall Jn.

HORNCASTLE 15
SPILSBY 20
Halton Holgate
Burgh le Marsh
SKEGNESS
Firsby **19**
Seacroft **21**
Havenhouse
Thorpe Culvert
Wainfleet

Sheffield →
Chesterfield →
Skellingthorpe
Hykeham **2**
Thorpe on the Hill
Swinderby
Waddington
Harmston
Navenby
Branston
Potterhanworth
Nocton & Dunston
Scopwick & Timberland
Digby
Blankney & Metheringham
Tattershall
Dogdyke
Coningsby
New Bolingbroke
Little Steeping
Midville
Tumby Woodside **17**
Stickney
Eastville
Old Leake
Sibsey **18**
Langrick

NEWARK
Doncaster ↑
Nottingham ↓
Claypole
Caythorpe
Ancaster
Leadenham
Hougham
Honington
Barkston **3**
GRANTHAM 4
Ruskington
SLEAFORD 9
Heckington
Helpringham
Swineshead
Hubbert's Bridge
BOSTON 13
Kirton
Algarkirk & Sutterton

Nottingham →
Sedgebrook
Great Ponton
Corby Glen
South Witham
Castle Bytham
Little Bytham
Raceby
Aswarby & Sedringham
Billingborough
Rippingale
Morton Road
BOURNE 7
Thurlby
Twenty **8**
Donington Road **10**
Gosberton
Pinchbeck
Surfleet
North Drove
SPALDING 11
Weston
Cowbit
HOLBEACH 12
Moulton
Whaplode
Fleet
Gedney
Long Sutton
Sutton Bridge
Counter Drain
Postland
Tydd

Melton Mowbray ←
Essendine
Braceborough Spa
Ryhall & Belmisthorpe
Tallington
Littleworth
Deeping St James
French Drove
King's Lynn →
Wisbech Peterborough →

N
STAMFORD 5
Uffington & Barnack **6**
Peakirk
March →
Leicester ←
PETERBOROUGH
London King's Cross →

	Great Northern Railway
	Great Central Railway
	Great Northern & Great Eastern Joint Railway
	Midland Railway
	Midland & Great Northern Joint Railway
	Lancashire, Derbyshire & East Coast Railway
	Isle of Axholme Joint Railway
	North Eastern Railway

● Stations open in 1989
○ Stations closed in 1989
6 Chapter Number

0 2 4 6 8 10 12 miles

(iv)

Lincolnshire and its Railways

Until recently Lincolnshire's railways had received little attention from writers and detailed information about the once extensive network could only be gleaned from company histories, particularly those dealing with the Great Northern Railway and Great Central Railway. Increased interest means that this situation is changing, with publications ranging from studies of individual branch lines to books on particular places or specific subjects.

However, this is the first work to take an overall look at both surviving and abandoned lines throughout the country – including the part which became South Humberside in 1974. Historical background has been kept to a minimum. Instead the book pays special attention to the character of the lines and examines distinctive features such as station architecture. At the same time an attempt has been made to capture the unique atmosphere of the surroundings and relate the railways to the districts they served.

LINCOLNSHIRE LANDSCAPE

The strongest and most persistent image of Lincolnshire to outsiders is one of flat fields stretching away to a broad horizon – classic Fenland scenery. But even a casual acquaintance of the county will begin to realise its diversity when reminded of the dune – backed holiday beaches of Mablethorpe, the lovely rolling Wolds west of Louth, the mighty cathedral overlooking Lincoln, the blast furnaces of Scunthorpe and the generations of trawlers which set sail from Grimsby. There is plenty of scope for variety. Nearly 50 miles separate the county boundary at Girton, west of Lincoln, from the North Sea at Skegness, and prior to the creation of Humberside in 1974 the old county stretched for 75 miles from Whitton, in the north, to Stamford in the south. Even the local dialect varies from a hint of Yorkshire at Grimsby to shades of East Anglia at Spalding. When London – Cleethorpes expresses travelled via Spalding, Boston and Louth they were only just over half way through their 158 mile journey as they entered Lincolnshire, and in 1970 the afternoon train spent over 2 hours of its 3½ hours running time in the county.

To some extent the common perception of Lincolnshire is valid, for low – lying farmland does indeed form a sizeable proportion of the total area. However, two north – south bands of higher ground presenting a steep slope to the west provide a marked contrast, and largely determined the overall shape of the railway network. **Lincoln Heath** is part of a great belt of limestone and ironstone extending from the North Yorkshire Moors to the Cotswolds. From cliffs overlooking the Humber at Alkborough to a broad spread of upland leading into Leicestershire, it rarely rises above 300ft, yet it proved a major obstacle to the construction and operation of the East Coast main line. It is breached by the River Witham at Lincoln and the resultant gap has always been a focal point for Lincolnshire railways. The **Lincolnshire Wolds** are part of an outcrop of chalk stretching from Flamborough Head on the Yorkshire coast to the Chiltern Hills and Salisbury Plain. They rise from the Humber estuary at South Ferriby near Barton on Humber, exceed 500 ft. near Caistor, and sink beneath the Fens at Spilsby. Within their folds are some of the most precious pieces of scenery in eastern England. With one exception railways avoided the high Wolds, although the gap at Barnetby resulted in a convergence of routes second only to Lincoln.

South – east Lincolnshire is dominated by the **Fens** – a huge expanse of levels lying just above or occasionally even just below high water mark. Railways in this area were cheap to build and

Shortly after mid-day on 3rd June 1964 a class WD 'Austerity' 2-8-0 blasted across Lincoln High Street with a heavy eastbound freight, to the frustration of factory workers returning home for their lunch hour. The mighty cathedral had been a symbol of stability for centuries, but the 1960s were to see dramatic changes in Britain generally and the railways in particular. Steam traction was about to disappear, and no doubt many people were pleased to see the end of it in the heart of the city. Although there were plenty of motor vehicles around, High Street was not completely clogged with them as is so often the case now, and it is interesting to note the number of cycles mingling with the Ford Anglias and Lincoln City Transport's AEC Bridgemasters. Photograph C.V. Middleton.

tended to run in straight lines, although the proliferation of level crossings proved an economic handicap. A finger of Fenland points along the **Witham Valley** towards Lincoln, and north of the city the **Ancholme Valley** completes the divide between the Heath and the Wolds as far as the Humber. Both valleys were used by railway routes in the 1840s. Away to the north – west, when the old county extended beyond the broad **Trent Valley**, an inhospitable wasteland was relieved by a slight rise known as the **Isle of Axholme.** The area seems almost alien to Lincolnshire, as did its very own railway. Finally there is the **Marsh**, a narrow strip of lowland fringing the North Sea. One of Lincolnshire's earliest railways ran throughout its length, but just as important were the branch lines which created and served the county's three main holiday resorts – Cleethorpes, Mablethorpe and Skegness.

THE RAILWAY NETWORK

The pattern of Lincolnshire's railway history, both in development and decline, tended to break the rules when compared with the general picture across the rest of England. The large tract of land covered by Lindsey, Kesteven and Holland experienced neither the pioneering days of horse waggonways nor the excitement of early steam locomotives and was still completely devoid of track at the end of 1845 when railways were firmly established in many areas. Yet within four years over 200 miles of line had been brought into use and apart from one short section this entire network was still carrying passenger trains 120 years later. Unlike most other rural areas, another substantial rise in track mileage occurred in the early 1900s when a whole series of railways began to serve the northern reaches of the county, largely   in connection with the development of Immingham Docks. Somewhat surprisingly, Lincolnshire remained virtually unscathed during the 1920s and 1930s when there were wholesale withdrawals of passenger services in many parts of the country. But the

relentless closure of individual stations and a handful of lines in the 1950s and early 1960s meant that the Beeching Report of 1963 had little immediate effect on the county, apart from the virtual wiping out of rural goods depots. Finally, and somewhat ironically, after the 1968 Transport Act had more or less stemmed the disintegration of the local rail network elsewhere, Lincolnshire lost the bulk of its system in 1970.

The sluggish start to railway construction in the county was partly attributable to the lack of coal and other known mineral resources, but also reflected the relative remoteness of this bulge of England between the Humber estuary and the Wash. There was no reason why lines linking expanding industrial areas inland should venture this far east. Although various railways schemes involving the county were mooted in the 1830s and even the 1820s, Lincolnshire had to wait until the 'Mania' of 1844–5 before receiving fruitful attention from speculators. This proved to be a turbulent business and even degenerated into fisticuffs at one Lincoln meeting. The conflict involved rival proposals for a direct London – York line and was further complicated by the frantic efforts of George Hudson, the self – styled 'Railway King', to protect his empire. This included both the Midland and York & North Midland companies which carried existing London – York traffic. In marked contrast the contemporary proposal to build a line from Sheffield to Grimsby and develop a deep water port progressed smoothly.

After the Great Northern was born out of the East Coast main line turmoil and the euphoria of the mid – 1840s had been tempered by a recession, Lincoln began to acquire a network of railways which were to revolutionise much of the county. In retrospect, the development of the system went through four distinct phases. The first period, from 1845 to 1854, began with the materialisation of Hudson's attempts to stifle potential competition. Useful as they are today, the Nottingham – Newark – Lincoln and Leicester – Stamford – Peterborough lines of the former

Midland Railway initially represented thrusts into territory earmarked for the GN route. The GN 'Lincolnshire Loop' from Peterborough to Spalding, Boston, Lincoln and Gainsborough, together with the East Lincolnshire route from Grimsby to Boston, and the Manchester, Sheffield & Lincolnshire Railway's Sheffield – Grimsby, Barnetby – Lincoln and Brocklesby/Harbrough – New Holland/Barton on Humber lines all opened in 1848–9. Most of Lincolnshire's good quality station architecture dated from this time. A Nottingham – Grantham connection (1850) and the GN 'Towns Line' from Peterborough to Grantham, Newark and Retford (1852) – the last link in the main line north – completed the basic network.

The second phase, from 1855 to 1870, saw the construction of numerous local lines built for a variety of reasons. Several market towns were rescued from their isolation by independent companies: Horncastle (1855); Sleaford (1857); Bourne (1860); and Spilsby (1868). The growing popularity of sea bathing at Cleethorpes and the beginning of iron smelting at Scunthorpe prompted new branches in 1863 and 1866 respectively. Between 1858 and 1866 there was a lot of activity in the extreme south – east as local railways began to exploit the fertile Fens, albeit with a route through to Norfolk in mind. Meanwhile the GN was busy filling gaps in that part of its territory under threat from the Great Eastern Railway, which was desperate to reach the South Yorkshire coalfield. Lines from Spalding to March, Honington to Lincoln, Gainsborough to Doncaster (all 1867) and Bourne to Sleaford (delayed for five years) were the result.

Phase three, from 1871 to 1890, was characterised by developments in the coastal area. Initially these were concerned with agriculture and harbours, but over the two decades south Lindsey's beaches were transformed into a holiday playground for workers from the industrial East Midlands. Railways were laid to Wainfleet (1871), Skegness (1873), Mablethorpe (1877) and Sutton on Sea (1886), whilst the Mablethorpe loop was completed in 1888. Two new

Lincolnshire once had numerous Great Northern branch lines presenting idyllic scenes such as this. N5 0-6-2 tank No.69258 paused at Ryhall & Belmisthorpe just inside the Rutland border with an Essendine to Stamford Town train on 24th June 1958. Photograph R.C. Riley.

lines were also built further inland and there could hardly have been a greater contrast between their respective fortunes. The Louth & Lincoln (1876) braved the high Wolds and was truly delightful, yet it proved a financial catastrophe. But the Great Northern and Great Eastern Joint route (1882), which finally gave the latter company access to Yorkshire, immediately became a new main line for both passenger and freight traffic.

The main focus of activity moved north for the final period, from 1891 to the outbreak of World War 1, although this phase began and ended with east – west lines – the last of many such schemes, most of them abortive. With the creation of the Midland & Great Northern Joint Committee and the opening of the Saxby – Bourne line in 1894, traffic between the Midlands and Norfolk began to flow in earnest. The hugely ambitious Lancashire, Derbyshire & East Coast Railway which envisaged docks at Sutton on Sea was never completed, but managed to reach Lincoln from the west in 1896. The Isle of Axholme Light Railway (opened 1900 – 10) served the bleak north – west of the county and the North Lindsey Light Railway (1906 – 10) helped to exploit iron reserves near Scunthorpe. Far more important was the Great Central's massive dock development at Immingham which resulted in a whole series of lines being laid between 1910 and 1912, including the Grimsby & Immingham tramway. Finally, retuning to east–west links, the Kirkstead & Little Steeping line across the Fens came in 1913, principally to help the GN cope with the phenomenal increase in seaside holiday traffic. With this sudden upsurge in new construction Lincolnshire's main rail network had reached its zenith, although many miles of industrial, agricultural and military track were subsequently opened.

The withering attacks on the system between 1950 and 1970 have left what at first appears to be an imbalance between north and south. In 1992 just 25 stations served 575,000 people in the 2300 sq. miles of present day Lincolnshire representing 17% of the original tally. At the same time the 400 sq. miles ceded to Humberside in 1974, population 305,000, has 20 stations – 51% of those once open (if the Grimsby & Immingham tramway halts are discounted). Furthermore, most former Great Central routes in the north survive whilst many ex–Great Northern lines in the south have been lifted. In reality, the railways reflect a fundamental contrast between the two areas. South Humberside has an industrial base with Immingham's docks and refineries and British Steel Scunthorpe providing a lot of traffic. The rest of Lincolnshire is predominantly agricultural and with large stretches of open countryside separating the scattering of market towns many lines were in financial trouble long before they closed.

Although Lincolnshire's railway network has remained more or less stable for a number of years, it would be wrong to rule out further changes. The division of BR's operations into Business Sectors in 1982 was followed by a steady reduction in government grants for Provincial Sector's unprofitable yet 'socially necessary' passenger services. With the privatisation of BR now on the agenda, there is a possibility that some loss–making routes may be eliminated altogether and recently, Gainsborough – Barnetby was seen as a test case for bus substitution. So, Grantham – Skegness, Peterborough – Lincoln – Doncaster, Lincoln – Barnetby, and Cleethorpes – Barton on Humber could be vulnerable. The proposed redevelopment of Cleethorpes seafront and the desire to eliminate Grimsby's level crossings pose further threats. But this is taking a pessimistic view. With environmental issues becoming increasingly important and a growing realisation that transport pressures cannot be eased soley by building more roads, is moving more towards the railways. In addition Regional Railways (Provincial's successor) is taking a more aggressive marketing stance. So Lincolnshire's surviving lines may well have a future. Although it does seem unlikely that there will be any actual line re–openings as in several other parts of the country.

Above. In marked contrast, the north of the county had numerous industrial areas. Class B1 4-6-0 No.61168 was about to pass under the trolleybus wires of Cleethorpe Road with a stopping train from Cleethorpes in the late 1950s as K2/2 No.61743 waited at the entrance to Grimsby Fish Docks. Photograph D.B. Swale.

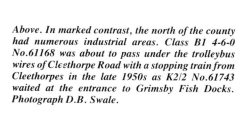

Below. Seaside excursions and extras ran over many Lincolnshire lines during the holiday season. B1 No.61210 on a summer-only train for Nottingham Victoria came face to face with a local diesel multiple unit at Mablethorpe during the summer of 1965. This station was one of the victims of the 1970 closures and virtually every trace of it has been swept away. Photograph D.B. Swale.

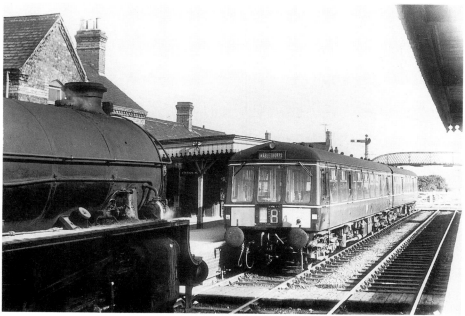

A cloudy but bright summer morning greeted ex-Great Central class D11/1 'Large Director' No.6670 MARNE as it drifted into Lincoln on 25th August 1956 with a train from Derby Midland. Fairburn class 4MT 2-6-4 tank No.42161 had a full head of steam ready for its imminent departure for Nottingham Midland. By this time 'St. Marks' appeared on the nameboards, the suffix having been added in September 1950 to distinguish the station from its former rival down the road. Inspiration for the name came from the building on the left. Complete reconstruction of the medieval St. Mark's church in 1871 produced the fine Victorian-gothic spire. The church was declared redundant in 1969 and despite strong and prolonged opposition it was demolished in 1972. Photograph J. Cupit.

Chapter 1

Lincoln St.Marks

The Lincoln Imp

Besides being an important commercial and industrial centre, Lincoln is one of the country's great historic cities and a major tourist attraction. Its origins go back two thousand years to the establishment of a Roman fort called Lindum Colonia on high ground overlooking the gap which the River Witham had carved through Lincoln Heath. Newport Arch, the fort's northern gateway, can still be seen. In 1086 William the Conqueror built a castle on almost the same site to subdue rebellious locals. Three hundred years later Lincoln had become one of the wealthiest cities in medieval England dominated by a majestic cathedral which is now regarded as one of the finest buildings in Europe. Centuries of stagnation followed the prosperity, but the coming of the railways changed all that.

A railway from Cambridge to Lincoln was suggested as early as 1821, and over the next quarter of a century more than fifty schemes involved the city, most of them dating from the mania years of 1844–5. But there was much talking and very little action until George Hudson lost his battle to block all proposals for a direct London – York line. With characteristic determination, he decided to reach Lincoln first, gain an advantage – and keep it. Work began on extending the Midland Railway from Nottingham in October 1845 and within ten months the 33 mile branch was complete. The official opening of Lincolnshire's first railway took place on 3rd August 1846 with the city in festive mood. One feature of the celebrations seems to have been persistent cannonfire, although one unfortunate soul managed to blow himself up in the process! In the evening Hudson and his guests feasted at the nearby Durham Ox Inn, but the Mayor and Corporation of Lincoln were not invited because of their partiality for the London – York projects.

When a public service of five trains each way between Nottingham and Lincoln commenced the following day, construction of a permanent station adjoining High Street had only just been started and it was several weeks before the impressive terminus began to take shape. The main block was built parallel to the arrival platform and had a long classical facade featuring fluted Ionic columns. All four tracks were sheltered by twin roofs supported by a row of decorative iron columns and finished off with slatted–timber gable end screens. On 18th December 1848 the Manchester Sheffield & Lincolnshire Railway reached Lincoln and formed an end-on junction with the line from Nottingham, thus creating a through station. Far more significant had been the arrival of the Great Northern Railway in Lincoln two months previously and the completion of its Peterborough – London line on 5th August 1850. Hudson had gone from the scene and in any case the Midland realised that it just could not compete.

So, the Nottingham – Lincoln branch assumed the role of a purely local link, remote from the company's thrusts towards St. Pancras, Manchester or Scotland, and this minor role continued for

Plain canopies replaced the overall roof in 1957 and the station took on a rather bleak, open look. One of the 2-car diesel multiple units built by Derby Works in 1956 for Lincolnshire local services negotiated the wide High Street level crossing on 25th October 1972. The empty stock, with E50006 leading, was heading for Lincoln diesel depot. Some of these railcars survived as class 114 into the 1990s. Photograph V.R. Webster.

well over a century. In September 1950 the suffix 'St.Marks' appeared on the nameboards to distinguish the station from its former rival down the road.

During the early 1960s St. Marks station still provided Lincoln with a good service to Newark, Nottingham and Derby. In 1961, for example, diesel multiple units departed hourly from 6.10 a.m. to 9.10p.m. for Derby Midland, the return workings arriving at Lincoln on the hour. At this time the line over High Street crossing saw very few passenger trains, although some of those that did use it were long distance workings – such as the summer Saturdays Cleethorpes to Sidmouth and Exmouth. The Beeching report of 1963 nearly put an end to all this, for it recommended complete closure of the Nottingham – Lincoln line. However, in 1965 BR decided to abandon the Grantham – Lincoln line instead and send traffic over a new connection at Newark between the former Midland route and the East Coast main line. The future of Lincoln's first railway was secure for the time being, although a dark cloud hung over St. Marks itself in view of the plans to divert trains into Central – the former Great Northern station.

On 5th October 1970 St. Marks enjoyed more than a reprieve: it became by far the more important of the two. All– stations locals to Nottingham and the recently introduced Cleethorpes – Newark Northgate semi–fasts continued as before but with the closure of the East Lincolnshire line through Louth and Boston, all Grimsby – London expresses came this was as well. Some effort was made to tidy up the station which had presented a bleak and neglected appearance since the overall roof was removed in 1957. Shortly after these improvements, detailed consideration was even given to the closure of Central. But in view of the passenger

services it offered, St.Marks was not really up to standard and must have given many visitors a poor first impression of the city. Central was better in all manner of ways, but diverting Nottingham and Newark trains into it was proving difficult. However, by 1982 a solution had been found. It was clear that traffic using the Lincoln avoiding line had declined so much that it could be abandoned and part of the embankment near Boultham Junction removed to make way for the required link. As a result, late on Saturday 12th May 1985 St.Marks dealt with its last passengers.

Within hours the signals protecting High Street crossing were removed and a memorial plaque bearing the names of Midland Railway employees who had perished in World War 1 was transferred to Central station three months later. After the track was taken up, archaeologists excavated the Carmelite friary which had occupied the site 700 years previously. Meanwhile, options for preserving the listed but decaying frontage were being explored. Planning permission for a shopping centre was granted in 1991, but by mid–1992 the site was still derelict.

a High Street
b Pelham St Flyover
c Durham Ox Jn.

d Holmes Yard
e GN Loco Shed
f GC Loco Shed

Market Rasen

Gainsborough

Pyewipe Jn.
West Holmes Jn.

Castle
Cathedral

Brayford Pool

Boultham Jn.

LINCOLN CENTRAL

Sincil Jn.

Boston

1985 Line

N

Lincoln St. Marks

Greetwell Jn.

Sleaford

Avoiding Line

0   ½ mile

Nottingham   Grantham

For a while the Nottingham to Lincoln line became a refuge for pensioned-off express passenger locomotives such as S.W. Johnson's 2-4-0s, the first of which were built in 1876 for the new Settle & Carlisle line. No.184 waited at Lincoln with the 3pm to Nottingham on 8th June 1926, a year before the engine was withdrawn. Photograph H.C. Casserley.

High Street Lincoln during the summer of 1902 was busy enough, but most people were walking and wheeled transport consisted largely of bicycles, handcarts and horse drawn wagons. The Lincoln Tramways Company's Bracebridge – St. Benedict's route of 1882 was also still horse operated. Electrification came in 1904 a year after the Corporation took it over, but the line was abandoned in 1929. St. Mark's church was prominent again, and even made an attempt to outshine the distant cathedral. The Midland station occupies the left hand side of this view and a cobbled area across the road pinpoints the connecting Great Central metals. Photograph National Railway Museum.

Ex-Great Central Atlantic class C4 No.2910 approaching Lincoln Central from the east with a long freight on 11th September 1948. The footbridge in the background is at Pelham Street crossing and prominent behind the train are Rustons factory and the Durham Ox pub. This particular railway route into the city was very complicated and involved Greetwell, Sincil and Durham Ox Junctions in quick succession. The last one controlled the rail level crossing with the St. Marks – Market Rasen line, the spur on to this from Central, and the road level crossing with Pelham Street. Photograph V.R. Webster.

Chapter 2

Lincoln Central

Lincoln's Heraldic Shield

By constructing the Fossdyke Canal and utilising the River Witham, the Romans firmly established east–west navigation between the Wash and the River Trent via Lincoln. Indeed, waterways provided the lifeblood for Lincoln's commerce for centuries, and the arrival of the Midland Railway had little effect on established trading patterns. But within a year construction work on the Great Northern 'loop' had commenced, the Witham and Fossdyke Navigations had passed into railway ownership, and boat proprietors faced the daunting prospect of goods trains running along a parallel route all the way from Boston to Gainsborough. Therefore it is perhaps surprising that commercial traffic on the waterways continued to flourish well into the 20th century and did not finally expire until 1972 – well after the railways had lost most freight to road transport.

On 17th October 1848 the section of 'loop' from Peterborough, Spalding and Boston opened with little ceremony at Lincoln. In marked contrast a feast at the Durham Ox, similar to that heralding the arrival of the Midland, took place on 18th December 1848 to celebrate the completion of the Manchester, Sheffield & Lincolnshire's Grimsby – Market Rasen – Lincoln line. The extension of the 'loop' through to Gainsborough followed on 9th April 1849. In just over 2½ years Lincoln had acquired railways radiating in four directions and from 1st August 1850 London was a mere 4 hours away thanks to the GN – fifteen years earlier the journey had been an 18 hour marathon by stagecoach.

By 1847 Lincoln had spread well beyond the medieval core of the city and its built–up area tumbled down across the Witham valley towards Bracebridge. So although the GN took advantage of open flood–prone common land for its approaches, the actual station site involved the demolition of a motley assemblage of cottages, workshops and stoneyards off Pelham Street. Lincoln High Street station was a lavish affair, totally out of character with the GN's frugal architectural policy and totally in harmony with the historic city it served. The main building, faced in grey bricks relieved by stone dressings, featured pointed arches, Tudor gables, a forest of tall chimneys and a Baronial tower boasting circular mock–Gothic windows. Frivolous details such as the curious stone shield overlooking the main platform were, for the GN, even more remarkable.

Even before the 'loop' opened, concern was

Platforms 1 to 4 at Lincoln Central were bays at the east end for local services to Grimsby, Skegness, Boston, Sleaford and Grantham. They were also used for parcels traffic as in this mid-1950s view of class D11/1 4-4-0 No.62660 BUTLER HENDERSON with a very junior footplateman. Platform 4 was and still is dominated by the fine tower of the main station building. Photograph John Clay.

expressed about the disruptive effect of two High Street level crossings. These fears were justified, for the GN gates were constantly opening and closing, and road congestion became a problem. The avoiding line, opened in 1882 as part of the Great Northern/Great Eastern joint railway (Chapter 10), took a lot of through freight and provided some relief. By 1925 the southward expansion of the city, combined with an increase in motor vehicles, had exacerbated the problem and prompted one councillor to condemn Lincoln's crossings as the worst in England. Numerous remedies were suggested over the years, including separate termini either side of High Street, a high–level line and station, and new spurs feeding an American–style 'Union' terminus elsewhere in the city. None came to fruition and the former GN crossing is still busy, although for much of the day High Street traffic is virtually at a standstill whether the gates are closed or not. Pelham Street crossing east of the station also became a major source of congestion, but fortunately there was enough room to build a bridge here, although the Durham Ox pub was demolished in the process.

Lincoln would undoubtedly have had a higher status in railway terms had it been on the main trunk route to the north, but despite its secondary nature the GN station has seen a rich variety of traffic in its 140 years history. GN and MS & L trains provided local services from the outset; Great Eastern and Lancashire, Derbyshire & East Coast locomotives became a familiar sight from the late nineteenth century; North Eastern and Lancashire & Yorkshire workings appeared before Grouping and diversions of named main line trains were not uncommon.

Following a period of uncertainty (Chapter 1), Lincoln Central has blossomed and is now one of the most delightful medium sized stations on BR. Despite the loss of services over the LD & EC to Chesterfield Market Place and Shirebrook in 1951 and 1955 respectively, the closure of the Grantham line in 1965, and the end of passenger traffic to Firsby in 1970, trains still run in four directions from the city – just as they did in 1849. On the passenger side 116 trains started, terminated or called at the station every weekday in 1992 and freight traffic notably the distribution of Humberside oil products, is a 24 hours a day operation.

LNER class B4 No.6104, a former Great Central 'Immingham' 4-6-0, crossing High Street with a westbound express in the 1930s. The old Great Northern stables are to the right. Photograph R.C. Riley.

Pelham Street flyover takes shape on 20th April 1957 as a Ford 'pop' and a flamboyant Commer coach wait for class V2 2-6-2 No.60948 to clear the crossing with a Newcastle – Colchester express. Photograph J. Cupit.

Lincoln-based class B1 4-6-0 No.1281 in fine condition and a rather grimy Boston J2 0-6-0 No.65016 standing at the High Street end of Platforms 7 and 8 respectively on 11th September 1948. The footbridge, canopies and gas lamps were vintage Great Northern and looked in need of some attention. Photograph V.R. Webster.

Just before mid-day on 25th July 1959 the Harwich Parkeston Quay – Liverpool Central boat train arrived at Lincoln Central behind Britannia Pacific No.70002 GEOFFREY CHAUCER as class K3 2-6-0 No.61972 paused with a York – Lowestoft express. Local diesel trains to Skegness, Boston and Grantham occupied the bay platforms while three light engines waited in the centre road for a path to the ex-GC loco shed. Photograph J. Cupit.

In February 1940 the gloom of wartime prevailed at Lincoln as elsewhere. With a backdrop of gas lamps masked in black and crew quarters protected by sandbags, ex-Great Central class B7 4-6-0 No.5185 took water prior to working a two coach train to Grantham in connection with a London express. Photograph V.R. Webster.

Earle's Field had passenger trains for less than five years but provided goods facilities for over a century. Ex-Great Northern class J6 0-6-0 No.64227 shunted Ambergate Yard at the original terminus of the line from Nottingham on 18th August 1953. The large AN & B & EJ station has now been demolished but a similar building in good condition can still be seen at Bottesford just over the Leicestershire boundary. Photograph J.P. Wilson.

Despite the gradients, demanding schedules have always been a feature of the 'Towns Line' and this was particularly apparent in Saltersford cutting just south of Grantham. On 7th May 1949 class A4 Pacific No.60021 WILD SWAN fresh from the loco shed, took over a Newcastle – King's Cross express at Grantham. With a 'green' fire, 15 coaches weighing some 500 tons and a strong tail wind, the smoke effect was spectacular as the engine attacked the 1 in 200 climb to Stoke summit. Photograph J.P. Wilson.

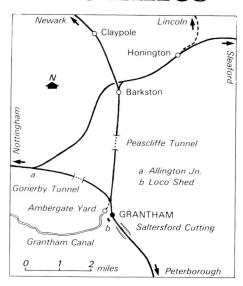

Sir Isaac Newton

Chapter 3
Grantham – The Lines

Some of Grantham's recent tourist information pamphlets have made much of the fact that Britain's first woman Prime Minister was born in the town. Understandably, they omitted to mention that some years ago a popular early morning radio show concluded that it was the most boring place in the country, judging by the response from local listeners! Whatever its present claims to fame, Grantham used to be a very exciting place as far as railways were concerned. For over a century it was an important locomotive–changing point on one of the fastest main lines in the world and witnessed a lot of railway history in the making.

Before the age of steam, Grantham developed in much the same way as other Lincolnshire market towns. During the 14th century the Great North Road brought trade and prosperity celebrated by the building of St. Wulfram's, the noble parish church with its needle–like 272 ft. spire. After the road was improved by the Turnpike Commissioners in 1725–38, stagecoach services boomed and several fine Georgian hotels replaced most medieval inns. From 1797 the Nottingham & Grantham Canal provided a valuable link and reduced the cost of transporting coal, manufactured goods and farm produce. Early railways missed the town and by 1845 the local economy was ailing, but the Great Northern Railway eventually provided salvation and a thriving engineering industry developed.

But the GN was not the first railway in Grantham. An ambitious scheme to link the East Midlands coalfield with the Lincolnshire coast gained parliamentary approval three weeks before the trunk route, and on 15th July 1850 the Ambergate, Nottingham & Boston & Eastern Junction Railway opened 22½ miles of track from Colwick (on the Midland's Lincoln branch east of Nottingham) to the canal basin at Earle's Field just west of Grantham. The AN & B & EJ purchased the Nottingham & Grantham Canal but abandoned the rest of its project through lack of capital. For five years the company ran a somewhat variable goods and passenger service while much wheeling and dealing took place as the GN and Midland fought to acquire it. On 2nd April 1855 the GN leased the line and inherited a motley assortment of diminutive engines. Passenger trains were diverted into the main Grantham station but Earle's Field continued to handle goods traffic.

After 17 years of grandiose east coast schemes which failed to materialise, followed by a further two years of bitter wrangling between more determined protagonists during and after the 'Railway Mania', the Great Northern was born in 1846 (see Introduction). But the vital 59¼

miles between Peterborough (Werrington Junction) and Retford via Grantham and Newark – the 'Towns Line' – was not opened for goods traffic until 15th July 1852 and passengers on 1st August. Kesteven's limestone uplands had made the Lincolnshire section a costly undertaking. From about 20 ft. above sea level at Werrington Junction, the line climbed up the Glen valley by means of an almost continuous succession of cuttings and embankments to 347 ft. at Stoke summit. A long descent through Stoke tunnel (880 yards), Grantham, Peascliffe tunnel (968 yards), and Claypole brought the tracks down to the Trent valley and below the 50 ft. contour again at Newark.

Within thirty years of the completion of the main line, a network of secondary railways had developed around Grantham. The route to Sleaford and Boston was built in 1857–9; a direct line to Lincoln via Leadenham opened from Honington on 15th April 1867; the Grantham avoiding line between Allington Junction and Barkston came into use on 29th October 1875; and the route through Melton Mowbray to Bottesford (which later carried a Leicester Belgrave Road – Grantham service) opened in 1879. The avoiding line was constructed primarily for freight, but rapidly became important for seaside holiday trains, whilst the Lincoln line proved a valuable diversionary route for east coast expresses. By the 1880s there was a considerable flow of coal traffic on to the main line from new GN branches in the Nottinghamshire Derbyshire colliery district, and locally the Belvoir and High Dyke branches assisted the exploitation of iron ore reserves on the Lincolnshire/Leicestershire border. Between 1878 and 1886 both the track layout and station accommodation at Grantham were expanded to cope with this increase in activity.

Fortunately Grantham has retained most of its railways. The Leicester service finished during 1953 and a few little–used stations such as Barkston, Sedgebrook and Hougham closed in 1955-57, yet even Beeching recommended the retention of the overall network. Despite his advice, the line to Lincoln Central was sacrificed on 30th October 1965 instead of the Newark – Lincoln St. Marks route. Regular freight traffic deserted the avoiding line in 1982, although seasonal Skegness

trains still use it.

Above all else, the fast passenger trains and their locomotives have provided the main source of railway interest at Grantham. Inevitably much of the glamour went with the demise of steam, but a modern east coast express at speed is still an impressive sight. Before the quest for excellence is examined in detail, it is worth noting one of the many humorous contrasts to all the speed and excitement. Many years ago a local farmer regularly became 'market merry' at Grantham, so it was customary for his drinking friends to steer him on to the last Lincoln service, leaving the Barkston porter to point him in the general direction of home. On one occasion the train paused near Peascliffe tunnel, and thinking he had reached the station the farmer opened the door and fell out. At Barkston there was just an empty compartment with the door swinging open. All traffic was stopped and men with lanterns embarked on a fruitless search. Just as a deputation arrived at the farmhouse to break the news, a much-sobered figure appeared and demanded to know why his wife was entertaining railwaymen in the small hours!

Navenby station on the Honington – Lincoln line was below the steep western edge of Lincoln Heath which can be seen in the distance in this 27th June 1933 view. Photograph H.C. Casserley.

On 16th September 1961 Gresley A3 Pacific No.60056 CENTENARY, then 36 years old, took charge of a Newcastle – King's Cross train at Grantham. It was fresh out of works with its newly fitted German style smoke deflectors, yet was destined to be withdrawn within eighteen months. The youngsters with duffle bags, Ian Allan 'Combines' and Brylcreemed short back and sides were witnessing the end of an era. Soon the Beatles records and mini skirts of the 'Swinging Sixties' would be a distraction from the diesel revolution on the main line. Photograph Gerald Morgan.

Chapter 4
Grantham – The Trains

St.Wulfram's

GN's first Chief Mechanical Engineer, designed a 4–2–2 similar to the Great Western Railway broad gauge flyers with a 2hr London–Grantham schedule in mind. Unfortunately No.215 proved to be a mechanical failure. Nevertheless, the GN gained a reputation for speed, and in 1867 the 'Engineer' magazine reported that a Sturrock 2–2–2 ran between London and Peterborough in 88 minutes with a 200 ton train. This remarkable 51 mph average speed was accomplished without the back up of continuous train braking and mechanical signalling.

Sturrock retired to lead the life of a country gentleman in 1866 and was succeeded by Patrick Stirling from the Glasgow & South Western Railway. His zeal for fast single–wheelers is legendary and he once described a four coupled engine at speed as like 'a laddie running with his breeks doon'. One of his 7ft 6in driving wheel 2–2–2s reached 86 mph, but it was the 53 8ft 4–2–2s built between 1870 and 1895 which captured the public's imagination with their greyhound–like appearance. From 1883 they regularly averaged 52 mph between Kings Cross and Grantham with the Manchester expresses, making these the fastest trains in the world for a while, and on 20th August 1895 – the last night of the 'Races to Aberdeen' – No 668 reached Grantham in 101 minutes, averaging 62½ mph. Such performances were achieved with lightweight trains of just over 100 tons, but No. 1006 – with a Grantham crew – had no less than 300 tons in tow when it averaged nearly 54 m.p.h. between London and Grantham in 1899. During these pioneering years a lot depended on the skill of the rugged individuals from Grantham shed, amongst

others, and it was in the Stirling era that a career on the footplate began to acquire its mystique.

Stirling died in office during 1895, by which time he had reluctantly allowed double–heading on the heavy dining car/corridor trains which were spelling the doom of his beloved Singles. His successor, H.A. Ivatt, had other ideas. The GN needed much larger engines and several batches of 4–4–0s were introduced as an interim measure. Even so, the concept of fast lightweight trains persisted and accordingly Ivatt designed 12 inside-cylinder 4–2–2s which proved to be the last single–wheelers built for Britain's railways. Meanwhile 4–4–2s were proving a great success in the USA, particularly on the Philadelphia & Reading Railroad's Atlantic City fliers and Ivatt was impressed. The first GN Atlantic appeared in 1898 and was based at Grantham for much of its experimental running. No. 990 *Henry Oakley* was Britain's most powerful express locomotive to date and was followed by a further 115 GN 4–4–2s, most of them with larger boilers. Grantham men did sound but unspectacular work with their Ivatt engines, but the excitement of the Stirling years had gone and other railways stole the limelight. Eventually the larger boilered Atlantics were fitted with augmented superheaters and proved valuable substitutes for failed larger engines. On one such occasion in 1936 No. 4404 averaged over 57 m.p.h. between Grantham and York with a 17–coach 585 ton train. They also put in some some sparkling performances on the LNER's Pullmans.

In 1911 Ivatt was succeeded by Nigel Gresley, one of the great names in British railway history. Previously he had been responsible for

Grantham is 105½ miles from Kings Cross and the shrinking journey time over the last 140 years reflects the constant drive to improve East Coast services. Initially most trains took between three and four hours – an average speed of about 30 mph – and even the diminutive 'Sharpie' 2–2–2s built for the GN's early operations in East Lincolnshire had a share of main line work. In 1853 Swindon–trained Archibald Sturrock, the

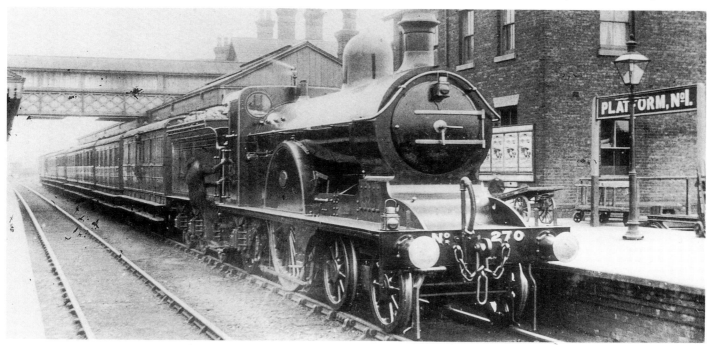

Great Northern Railway No.270, one of Ivatt's inside cylinder 4-2-2s, on a lightweight express bound for King's Cross in the early 1900s. The long demolished two storey house at the south end of platform 1 was one of the original GNR buildings. Photograph courtesy V.R. Webster.

15

modernising the GN's carriage stock – a daunting prospect in view of the legacy of six–wheelers left by Stirling. Many were converted into articulated bogie sets, although a number remained, and shamefully the LNER used them to strengthen expresses. During 1929 one writer travelled from Grantham to King's Cross in such a vehicle at the very end of the train and described the descent of Stoke bank at 88 m.p.h. as 'hardly equalled by a rough channel crossing'! Gresley's appointment coincided with the swansong of the Stirling Singles: No. 1003, the last active survivor, was withdrawn in 1915. His locomotive career began in a competent yet unspectacular way with a series of 2–6–0s, but in 1922 his first two Pacifics emerged from Doncaster Works resplendent in GN livery. As class A1 (not to be confused with the later Peppercorn engines) these 4–6–2s continued to appear after the Grouping and Grantham received its initial allocation in 1923. Their arduous duties included heavy sleeping car expresses and they were often in service for 12 hours at a time. Nevertheless the A1s were outshone by Great Western Railway 4–6–0 No. 4079 *Pendennis Castle* in the 1925 exchanges and modifications were clearly necessary. Improved valve gear helped – in 1932 the 7.50 a.m. from

Leeds was allowed just 100 minutes from Grantham to King's Cross (average 63 m.p.h.) and in 1933 a Grantham A1 took a 660 ton 19–coach train from Doncaster to Peterborough in 85 minutes (average 56 m.p.h.). Higher pressure boilers with larger superheater also became standard and rebuilt engines, together with new ones, became the familiar class A3. Undoubtedly the most famous early Gresley Pacific was No. 4472 *Flying Scotsman* which achieved the first non–stop King's Cross – Edinburgh run in 1928 and the first officially–recorded 100 m.p.h. maximum speed in 1934.

The late 1930s were especially exciting at Grantham. In 1935 Gresley introduced his A4 Pacifics for the *Silver Jubilee* express. With their streamlining, chime whistles and silver–grey livery these magnificent engines caused quite a sensation and the new trains revived the flagging image of the railways among the general public. As the climax of a demonstration run with 7 coaches on 27 September 1935 No.2509 *Silver Link* would have reached Grantham in about 77 minutes had it not caught up with a train which left London 40 minutes earlier. During the journey it averaged 100 m.p.h. for 43 miles and twice reached 112 m.p.h. The fastest run by an

A4 in ordinary service was on 28th September 1937 when No. 4492 *Dominion of New Zealand* reached King's Cross in 82 minutes 6 seconds after passing Grantham (over 77 m.p.h. average). The pinnacle of achievement came with the special attempt on 3rd July 1938 when No. 4468 *Mallard* reached 126 m.p.h. between Little Bytham and Essendine, setting a world steam speed record which is unlikely to be bettered.

All the streamliners, including the bright Garter blue *Coronation* and *West Riding* expresses of 1937, passed non–stop through Grantham and although two A4s were allocated there in 1938, the shed remained a stronghold of the A1s. World War 2 brought very heavy trains, reduced maintenance and coal described by one fireman as 'broken gravestones', yet Grantham's A1s sometimes performed scarcely credible feats. In 1940 No. 2549 *Persimmon* took a packed 23 coach 860 ton train from Peterborough to London in 96 minutes at an average speed of over 47 m.p.h. A V2 2-6-2 did a similar journey with 25 coaches, although no speed records were broken on this occasion!

The GN main line was also noted for fast freights, and although these understandably received less acclaim than the prestige passenger

Although the Ivatt Atlantics were relegated to secondary duties as new 4-6-2 and 2-6-2 express engines appeared, they still had their moments of glory in the 1930s. On a day when the rostered Pacific failed, No.4436 assisted by a 4-4-0 made a determined start from Grantham with a heavy Edinburgh – London express. the Atlantic survived into BR ownership as class C1 No.62866. Photograph T.G. Hepburn.

No.4472 FLYING SCOTSMAN on the up 'Flying Scotsman' express at Grantham in the early 1930s. Photograph courtesy Vic Forster.

A4 Pacific No.2509 SILVER LINK passing Barkston with the up 'Silver Jubilee' in the mid 1930s. Photograph T.G. Hepburn.

trains they were part of an impressive operation. In 1936 Gresley introduced his class V2 *Green Arrow* 2–6–2s which helped to maintain the reputation of the fast Scottish goods. Far less glamorous were the Colwick – Peterborough coal trains and High Dyke – Scunthorpe iron ore workings, usually headed by big class O2 2–8–0s.

Local passenger services tended to be out of the limelight as well. They were a refuge for retired express engines and by 1913 the once-proud Stirling Single No. 1006 (see earlier) was sub-shedded at Leicester Belgrave Road for the pedestrian service to Peterborough – work 'at which a London bus horse would have turned up its nose' according to a contemporary writer. As the number of Pacifics and V2s increased, it was the turn of the Ivatt 4–4–0s, and then the Atlantics to be relegated. The last Atlantic, No. 62822, remained active in the Grantham area until 1951, but by that time former express engines from elsewhere were employed, including ex–Great Eastern 4–6–0s and ex–Great Central 4–4–0s.

Sir Nigel Gresley, as he had become, died in office during 1941 and Edward Thompson took over as CME, followed by A.H. Peppercorn from 1946 to Nationalisation. Wartime and immediate post–war conditions meant thatGresley's successor had to design easily maintained locomotives which were less susceptible to neglect. The best of these were Peppercorn's class A1 4–6–2s which have been described as Britain's most underrated Pacifics. Grantham received six A1s in 1951 and although their running was rarely spectacular they proved reliable and very economical. They were replaced by elderly Gresley A3s in the late 1950s and at first Grantham crews were depressed. But the old–timers had been fitted with Kylchap double blast pipes and could do all the work that was asked of them. In fact with their A3s the men ensured that steam trac-

tion had a brilliant finish at Grantham. In 1959 the up *Heart of Midlothian* loaded to 500 tons at weekends and was allowed 185 minutes between Newcastle and Grantham (over 52 m.p.h. average) with two intermediate stops. Furthermore, the A3s were known to pull back over 17 minutes of delay during the journey and still arrive at Grantham early.

English Electric Type 4 No.D207 from Hornsey depot was in charge of the northbound *Talisman* on 25th August 1958 and heralded the first intensive use of diesels on the GN main line. Engine–changing became less common at Grantham after 1961 and the shed closed on 7th

September 1963. In June 1964 A3 No. 60106 *Flying Fox* had the honour of being the last steam locomotive to haul the *Flying Scotsman* when it replaced a failed diesel. After 114 years it was indeed the end of steam at Grantham. The early Type 4s proved somewhat unreliable and in any case were no match for an A4 in fine fettle with an energetic fireman. Instead, the key to the future was a big American–looking diesel powered by naval gunboat engines and sporting a gaudy livery of pale blue garnished with yellow and silver stripes. In 1959 the prototype Deltic stormed up Stoke bank at 80 m.p.h. and when one of the 3300 h.p. Type 5 production models

Thompson class L1 2-6-4 tank No.67800 waited at Grantham on 24th June 1958 with a train for Nottingham Victoria. The J39 0-6-0 beyond was on an eastbound local service. Photograph R.C. Riley.

Ex-Great Central class D11/1 No.62670 MARNE was working a stopping train from Grantham to Lincoln Central on this summer Saturday in 1954. Meanwhile class J6 0-6-0 No.64178 headed a service for Nottingham Victoria. The motive power depot and coaling tower were prominent in the background. Photograph John Clay.

worked the southbound *Talisman* instead of an A4 on 12th June 1961 a new era had finally dawned. The Deltics were quite happy whisking along a 600 ton train at 90 m.p.h. for long distances and even breasted Stoke summit at 88 m.p.h. with the 460 ton 'Yorkshire Pullman'. As a result, June 1962 saw unprecedented East Coast accelerations. As more sections of track were cleared for 100 m.p.h. running the Deltics constantly broke their own records. In 1962 they were taking 92 minutes between King's Cross and Grantham with 11 Mk 1 coaches (69 m.p.h. average) but by 1980 the same journey with 9 Mk 2s was down to 71 minutes (90 m.p.h. average). Above all they were locomotives of character and their immense bulk, bulging contours and sonorous boom commanded considerable affec-

tion. So there was an ecstatic farewell on 2nd January 1982 when 55022 *Royal Scots Grey* hauled the King's Cross – Edinburgh grand finale.

The Deltics had given way to the now-familiar High Speed Trains or Inter–City 125s. By the early 1970s BR had concluded that trains capable of sustained 125 m.p.h. running on existing track were essential to stave off motorway competition. The prototype HST touched 143.2 m.p.h. between York and Darlington on 12th June 1973 and clearly the designers had come up with a winner. On 20th March 1978 an HST first took over a Deltic turn and after much preparatory trackwork another dramatic speed–up of East Coast services was announced for May 1979. On 27th September 1985, exactly 50 years after *Silver Link* made its epic run, an attempt was made

on the world diesel speed record. Specially selected power cars 43038 and 43158 with five coaches averaged 115.4 m.p.h. from Newcastle to King's Cross and with the Valenta engines screaming at maximum revs, the speedometer momentarily touched 145 m.p.h. during the descent of Stoke bank. Some East Coast HSTs had a working day of no less than 21 hours and after a troublesome period during 1983–5 are now one of BR's most reliable traffic units.

On 27th July 1984 the London – Leeds/Edinburgh electrification scheme was authorised and eventually it was decided that this would be the debut for BR's flagship of the future – the Inter–City 225s. The proposed class 91 locomotives, publicised as Electras, had a daunting technical specification. No less than 6300 h.p. had to be packed into an 80 tonne machine; they had to be kind to the track at 140 m.p.h.; and besides keeping to 4 hr. King's Cross – Edinburgh daytime passenger schedules they would be required to haul heavy overnight freights with Channel Tunnel implications paramount. On 5th February 1986 BR and GEC chiefs signed the Electra contract, with the latter having until October 1989 to get the sophisticated electronic control system right. No. 91001 was handed over to BR on 14th February 1988, an exhaustive programme of experimental running commenced, and the same locomotive was the first of the class to enter revenue-earning service on 3rd March 1989. 'Modern Railways' described the Electra as a 'demon–quick machine' – when running light they will accelerate from 0 – 75 m.p.h. in 20 seconds. Class 91s may be far removed from the 8 ft. Singles and A4s, but a lot of thought has gone into their external appearance and consequent public image – Stirling and Gresley would have approved! The full East Coast electrified service between King's Cross and Edinburgh began on 8th July 1991.

Grantham shed on 24th June 1958 with resident C12 4-4-2 tank No.67397 and a guest J39 0-6-0 No.64885 from Doncaster. Photograph R.C. Riley.

Deltic No. D9006 prior to naming droned through Grantham with the up 'Tees-Tyne Pullman' on 31st August 1964. Photograph Roger Hockney.

Standard class 4MT 4-6-0 No.75039 heading the early evening stopping service from Peterborough East to Leicester London Road out of Stamford tunnel and into Town station on 10th August 1963. Photograph P.H. Wells.

Stamford Town station blended in beautifully with the historic skyline and the only incongruous touches were the sheds and chimney of industrial premises near the goods yard. On the right ex-LMS 2-6-2 tank No.41214 waited at the rear of the Seaton push-pull 'Motor Train' in the bay platform. The date was 31st May 1958. Photograph R.C. Riley.

Also on 31st May 1958, class C12 4-4-2 tank No.67394 was in charge of an Essendine train at Stamford Town. At the time the station was still dominated by a lofty grain warehouse and large stone goods shed. Both of these have gone, but the Syston & Peterborough passenger building is as elegant as ever. Photograph R.C. Riley

Stamford Town

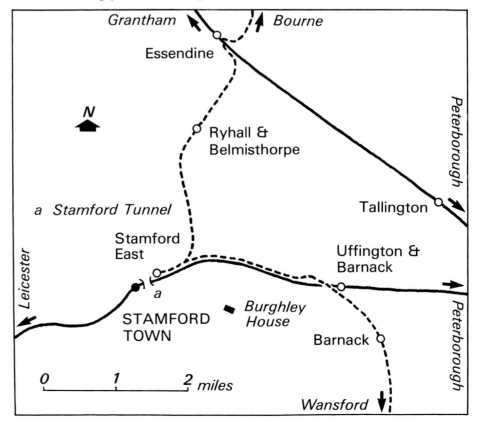

with their Tudor Gothic windows are set off by a three–bay entrance arcade and a delightful tower with its octagonal turret and 'SPR' weather vane. Despite these facilities, Stamford never really developed industrially as a result of its railways – a legacy of Lord Exeter's intransigence at a crucial time. Perhaps this was as well, for nowadays the town is justifiably proud of its untainted pre–Victorian heritage.

Through coal and freight traffic has always been important and for a while some of the former was hauled by the huge LMS Beyer–Garratt 2–6–6–2s. Apart from the Seaton shuttle and the westbound Harwich-Birmingham 'Continental' which came this way between the wars, most passenger trains were all–stations locals between Leicester and Peterborough. Long ago they were hauled by Midland 2–4–0s and 4–2–2 'Spinners' which eventually gave way to Midland, then to LMS 4-4-0s. In BR days there was a variety of motive power, with locomotives from March shed taking turns with demoted main–line engines and new standard types. For years the pattern of passenger services at Stamford Town remained basically the same, but on 4th March 1957 a new destination appeared on the timetable. Unfortunately, the addition of Essendine resulted from the closure of Stamford's other station rather than an expansion of the network, and in any case the service was withdrawn altogether just over two years later.

In 1963 the Syston & Peterborough route came near to extinction itself when Beeching advised complete closure to passengers. Fortunately for Stamford, the withdrawal of Northampton – Peterborough trains in 1964 followed by those between Rugby and Peterborough two

years later meant that certain long distance services were diverted over the line and its future prospects brightened somewhat. The only local casualty was the link to Seaton which finished with the Rugby – Peterborough line on 4th June 1966 and had the honour of being the last steam push–pull operation in the country. Diesel traction took over completely at Stamford, but all too often the quality of service was abysmal. Passengers making the 176 mile journey from Birmingham to Norwich sometimes had to endure nearly 4½ hours aboard a multiple–unit designed for local journeys, and on occasions when the toilet was out of order, travel by train became decidedly unattractive. The increased use of class 31 diesels and main-line coaches did improve matters substantially.

From May 1986 new class 150 Sprinters began to work some Birmingham – Cambridge services through Stamford, although the Norwich services were still formed of class 31 diesels hauling demoted 1st class Mk 2 coaches. From May 1988, Provincial Sector's class 156 Sprinters took over long distance services and in June 1991 the Regional Railways class 158 flagship appeared on certain Birmingham – East Anglia trains calling at Stamford. The line remained an important artery for freight including ECC stone from Croft to East Anglia and Castle Cement traffic from Ketton. Most present day travellers are unaware of the threat to Stamford's rail services in the 1960s and take the station for granted. Sleepy office girls on the early morning train to Peterborough and executives returning from London are considerably more fortunate than their counterparts in most other Lincolnshire market towns.

Stamford is one of the most attractive towns in England and it can thank Lincoln 'long wool' sheep for many of its mellow stone buildings. In medieval times local woollen cloth was renowned throughout Europe, and as the merchants became wealthy several of them became benefactors. They funded the lovely almshouses and several fine churches, notably St. Mary's with its magnificent tower and spire. A period of decline followed, but in the heyday of stagecoaches on the Great North Road Stamford prospered again and began to acquire many elegant Georgian buildings. There was much merrymaking at the inns, including the George which put up a huge gallows spanning the street to remind highwaymen that they were unwelcome. The Marquess of Exeter, resident of nearby Burghley House and owner of most of Stamford, adopted a similar attitude towards the Great Northern Railway in 1847. However, just prior to this stand he had been quite happy to allow the Midland Railway's Syston & Peterborough branch to pass through the town, and almost a century and half later it continues to do so.

Like the Nottingham–Lincoln line, the Syston & Peterborough was another of George Hudson's counter measures against the GN. Its eastern section opened on 2nd October 1846 as far as a temporary station at Water Street on the eastern edge of Stamford. Because of the famous conflict with Lord Harborough at Saxby, the Melton Mowbray – Stamford section, including the line through Stamford itself, was not opened for goods traffic until 20th March 1848, with passenger services commencing on 19th June. The Marquess of Exeter would not permit the Midland to make a level crossing with the Great North Road, so the railway was forced to tunnel through rising ground at one corner of Burghley Park and quite rightly made little visual impact on Stamford.

A remarkably fine range of station architecture was to be found on the Syston & Peterborough line and Sancton Wood's asymmetrical composition at Stamford was the best of all. From the approach road and platforms it makes an immediate impact, yet it is on a modest, almost miniature scale. The different–sized gable ends

Class 4F 0-6-0 No.43938 from Saltley shed in Birmingham had just left Stamford tunnel and was heading east on the Midland line when it was photographed passing the approach to Stamford East on 31st May 1958. This was the site of the temporary Water Street terminus from 1846 to 1848. Photograph R.C. Riley.

Ryhall and Belmisthorpe, the intermediate station on the Stamford & Essendine line, was far more modest than Stamford East, but its single storey building still featured prominent Elizabethan chimneys. On 24th June 1958 it basked in the warmth of a gorgeous summer day. Photograph R.C. Riley.

Chapter 6

Stamford East

Burghley House

Burghley House was completed in 1585 and is a magnificent example of Elizabethan splendour. Treasures such as the Heaven Room can now be admired by tourists whilst the landscaped park provides a noble setting for the famous horse trials. In 1847 the 7th Marquess of Exeter probably took his stately home for granted, for he was preoccupied with his political career. Bearing in mind the social changes being brought about by industrialisation, Lord

Exeter was convinced that his parliamentary future depended on Stamford remaining just as it was. Having a major railway line on its doorstep would have the opposite effect, so the Great Northern was encouraged to pass well to the east. Local traders despaired, and when the trunk route was completed in 1852, the Marquess began to regret his obduracy. In order to make amends, he promoted a link with the GN and his Stamford & Essendine Railway opened without ceremony on 1st November 1856. The Midland refused to let S & E trains use its facilities, so a terminus was built in Water Street near the site of the temporary Syston & Peterborough station. In an ill–fated attempt to provide better connections with London, a branch towards Peterborough was proposed, but this materialised on 9th August 1867 as a somewhat irrelevant line to Wansford.

The Marquess of Exeter's railway had a lively history. Initially it was worked by the GN which lost money in the process and eventually termin-

ated the agreement. So from 1st January 1865 the S&E began to run its own trains using second hand engines and coaches – some of the latter proudly displaying Lord Exeter's coat of arms. The GN resumed responsibility for the Essendine branch, together with the new Wansford line, on 1st February 1872 and before long through coaches from King's Cross to Stamford were being 'slipped' off some non–stop expresses at Essendine. Meanwhile, some drivers setting off for Wansford were trying to emulate their main––line colleagues by racing Midland trains on the parallel tracks out of Stamford. Complaints from passengers ended this practice before an accident occurred, but operations on the S & E were certainly not without incident. Level crossing gates were demolished, a train rammed the buffers at Stamford, and one engine toppled into the River Welland, achieving immortality as the 'Welland Diver'.

Considering the Marquess of Exeter's involvement with the line and the Victorian passion for

Stamford East was a neat and compact terminus, albeit slightly cramped in places. In dull weather on 18th September 1954, C12 No.67357 stood at the former Wansford platform as sister engine No.67365 waited with an Essendine train. With the Midland line just beyond the goods shed and the River Welland immediately to the right, there was little room for expansion, had traffic levels demanded it. This problem never arose, and nowadays the site of the platform is a courtyard in Welland Mews. Photograph V.R. Webster.

reviving earlier styles of architecture, it is hardly surprising that Burghley House provided inspiration for the S & E station in Stamford. William Hurst's handsome stone building could have been a Tudor nobleman's house; in reality it was one of the most charming railway termini in England. Burghley House displayed the balustrades, decorative gables, large showy chimneys and carved crests fashionable in great Elizabethan mansions, and all these features were present in the station design. Everything from the prominent tower to the smallest window was executed with considerable attention to detail. Although the booking hall was modestly proportioned internally, its hammerbeam roof culminated in a lantern, so the effect was light and airy. The S & E was understandably proud of its station and for forty years coaches were towed into the platforms so that soot from the engines would not sully the overall roof. Even the goods shed was built of grey limestone and was totally in keeping with the town. At Ryhall & Belmisthorpe the station house was a pleasant rustic cottage, and Barnack and Wansford Road stations on the later branch were truly delightful. Tudor touches appeared again and the S & E's penchant for big decorative chimneys even extended to the tiny weighbridge offices.

For most people, a journey from Stamford to London began with a trip on the Essendine local at the time the S & E lost its independence to the LNER on 1st January 1923. The Wansford line had never been more than an obscure rural branch, and as such it had a lot of character but precious little income. So the withdrawal of its passenger services as early as 1st July 1929 came as no surprise, although total closure a couple of years later seemed rather premature and met with a certain amount of opposition from farmers. Business carried on as usual at the Water Street terminus and even after nationalisation there were few changes. The buildings received a lick of regional bluish–green paint, the station name was altered from Stamford to Stamford East on 25th September 1950, and new numbers together with a lined–out livery appeared on the faithful class C12 4–4–2Ts which had served the line since the 1920s.

The remarkable booking office at Stamford East featured a hammerbeam roof and a balcony giving access to the company's offices. There was quite a contrast between the light, almost frivolous, wrought ironwork railings and the sombre carvings in the dark woodwork. Photograph courtesy D.L. Franks.

A panorama of the approach to Stamford East on 31st May 1958. As at Stamford Town, the railway buildings blended in well with the grey stone houses nearby. Photograph R.C. Riley.

Before long, retention of the terminus could no longer be justified and from 4th March 1957 trains were diverted into Stamford Town over an existing connection with the adjacent Midland line. Finally, a class N5 0-6-2 tank, No. 69292, scrawled with chalk tributes to the doomed 'Bread & Onion line' hauled the last Stamford – Essendine trains on 13th June 1959.

Goods traffic to Essendine barely outlived the passenger service, although Stamford East retained its yard which was served by a trip working from the Midland depot. This facility was withdrawn on 4th March 1963, but a little bit of the S & E lingered on for another six years in the form of a long siding to Blackstone's agricultural engineering works alongside the Ryhall road. This firm was a major employer in Stamford and until the 1950s chartered special trains to take its workers and their families for day excursions. Meanwhile the terminus – which was without its platform but otherwise complete – was taken over by a road haulage firm and much of the S & E character remained. Fortunately, the latest development looks like preserving the station block and goods shed for the foreseeable future. In 1987 a range of retirement bungalows, apartments and luxury homes known as Welland Mews was built on the site and the former railway structures were incorporated in the design.

Ex-Great Central class N5 0-6-2 tank No.69258 worked the Stamford & Essendine line on 24th June 1958. Duties included the local goods to Essendine. Photograph R.C. Riley.

No.69258 worked back from Essendine with the branch passenger train to Stamford Town on 24th June 1958. East station had closed to passengers by this time and the train was using the crossover between Great Northern and Midland metals. The GN signals had been replaced by newer equipment, but a fine Midland specimen still protected the junction. Photograph R.C. Riley.

Stamford was a sub-shed of 35A New England at Peterborough and No.69258 rested outside the diminutive structure on 24th June 1958. All the details of a classic branch line depot are present – the coaling stage with its crane, lamp and wagons of loco coal, the water tank on the roof and the water crane with its brazier, the sand furnace chimney, and the little pile of firebox rakings which had been barrowed out of the ash pit. Photograph R.C. Riley.

The 'Leicesters' were heavy trains in summer, but out of the holiday season they were much reduced in length. Ex-Great Eastern class B12/3 4-6-0 No.61533 blasted out of Bourne with a winter timetable 5-coach Yarmouth Beach – Leicester London Road train on 25th March 1950. Most of the train consisted of modern LMS-designed corridor stock. The tablet catcher for use on the long single track sections of the M&GN can be seen at the front of the tender. Bourne loco shed can be glimpsed to the left of the engine and the Red House is above the last coach. No.61533 was signalled for the Saxby line by West Junction box and the arm at danger controlled the Essendine line. Photograph J.P. Wilson.

Chapter 7

Bourne

Grimsthorpe Saracen's Head

Nine miles north east of Stamford, where the undulations of Kesteven give way to an expanse of flat fen, the Bourne Eau bubbles out of the limestone and a small settlement grew up. Hereward the Wake sought refuge here during his rebellion against the Normans and the village grew substantially after a great Augustinian abbey was founded in 1138, the church of which survives. One of the monks achieved fame by pioneering writing which could be understood by commoners. Today Bourne is a compact town centred on a small market square at the meeting point of roads from Grantham, Sleaford, Spalding and Peterborough. There are plenty of fine Georgian brick houses dating from the days when it was a stopping place for the London – Lincoln stagecoach, and the inns and traders were still prosperous when the Great Northern main line opened through Little Bytham, five miles away to the west.

A horse bus met the trains at Tallington, east of Stamford, but as the stagecoaches faltered it was clear that Bourne really needed a railway of its own. The first branch line in the area terminated 3¼ miles from the town and therefore did little to help. It was the delightfully ramshackle Edenham & Little Bytham Railway built in 1856 by Lord Willoughby de Eresby to connect his Grimsthorpe Castle estate with the GN. Shortly afterwards, local interests set up the Bourne & Essendine Railway which opened on 16th May 1860 and provided the required link with the main line 3¾ miles south of Little Bytham. For four years the company struggled on in poverty until bought out by the GN, which had always worked the branch. On 1st August 1866 trains began to run on the Spalding & Bourne Railway. Although the company was promoted independently, a complicated series of working arrangements and amalgamations eventually leading to the formation of the Midland & Great Northern Joint Railway had already started and in time involved this line. Meanwhile a threatened invasion of its territory by the Great Eastern Railway was causing anguish in the GN boardroom. Steps were taken to consolidate the network and one outcome was the Bourne – Sleaford line opened on 2nd January 1872. Finally the newly-formed M & GN had a long route from Norfolk but no direct connection with the industrial Midlands, so the Bourne – Saxby line was built to fill the gap and duly opened on 1st May 1894. Bourne then became a four-way junction and a place of some significance on the railway network.

Many railway companies opted for the Tudor style when building their stations – but this is the genuine article. The Red Hall was used as Bourne station for nearly a century, but had just closed when photographed on 9th July 1959. Photograph John Bonser.

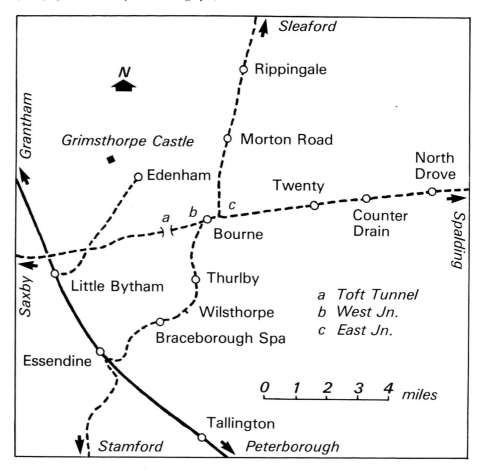

a Toft Tunnel
b West Jn.
c East Jn.

As elsewhere in Lincolnshire, the railways stimulated farming activity around Bourne and the substantial goods depot became a focal point for agricultural transport needs. Everything from fertilizer to farm machinery came in, whilst food-stuffs to satisfy the requirements of growing industrial towns and cities were dispatched. There was one rather special crop: Bourne's abundant supply of pure spring water was ideal for growing watercress, supplies of which were regularly sent to London markets. Nearby villages such as Thurlby and Rippingale, which had always looked to Bourne, also benefitted considerably from their local stations. Long-distance passenger traffic began to dominate the scene once the M & GN through route became established. A summer–only Birmingham – Leicester – Yarmouth service began almost immediately and by 1902 the 'Leicesters' were operating throughout the year with through coaches from added Nottingham and Derby. Before long there was a train from Leeds, and through coaches from Liverpool and Manchester via Nottingham.

Nor surprisingly, the Edenham & Little Bytham Railway closed first, but its demise was exceptionally early – October 1871 for passengers and completely within ten years. Despite serving the most populated area, the Sleaford branch was a purely local operation and passenger trains finished on 22nd September 1930. Bourne's connection with the main line might have gone shortly afterwards had World War 2 not intervened, and the Essendine service lasted until 16th June 1951 when the branch closed completely. Meanwhile four dozen brand new Ivatt 2–6–0s in the 43XXX series were gradually being drafted on to the M & GN to replace the ex–LNER engines which had kept services going following the withdrawal of the route's own motive power in the late 1930s. However, the loss of freight as well as local passenger traffic to road transport and the unacceptable cost of keeping the M & GN open just for busy summer Saturdays brought about its closure, together with Bourne station, on 28th February 1959. Through services subsequently travelled via Peterborough. Goods traffic finally ceased on 5th April 1965 but maintenance levels were kept to a minimum and Bourne's railway suffered a lingering death.

Bourne station had a unique claim to fame, for part of it was by far the oldest building in railway use. Ever on the lookout for ways of saving money, the Bourne & Essendine purchased the early 17th century Red Hall instead of constructing a new station house. It was once the home of Sir Everard Digby, and has often been incorrectly cited as the place where the Gunpowder Plot was hatched. For a while it became a school for young ladies, but was derelict before the B & E carried out restoration work. A single platform was sufficient initially, then a second one was added for the Sleaford branch. Wholesale changes were made when the M & GN took over, and from 1894 the station consisted of a long curving island platform with a range of GN–style buildings featuring a generous canopy. A locomotive shed, turntable, various sidings and the large goods shed completed the fairly extensive layout at Bourne. In BR days the Red Hall lost its grand stone chimneys and generally became dilapidated again. Demolition of such an historic building was unthinkable however, so rehabilitation was undertaken and the mansion is now in the care of Bourne United Charities. A well–kept lawn occupies part of the actual station site. The goods shed has found other uses and is now served by lorries rather than railway wagons.

Access to the 1894 island platform at Bourne was via a footbridge and this proved to be a fine vantage point, as shown by this view westwards on 4th October 1958. The substantial engine shed and turntable are in the background and a corner of the Red House garden occupies the right foreground. Away in the distance the limestone ridge which necessitated Toft Tunnel rises to form the skyline. Photograph Barry Hilton.

Considering their imminent demise, the platform buildings looked in good condition on 4th October 1958 – although the Red House was in a sorry state and had been shorn of its chimneys. Goods traffic had also declined and the impressive depot was underused. However, a feature of all these 1958 views is the general tidiness of railway property at the time – including the weed-free areas between the tracks. Photograph Barry Hilton.

The view from the end of the platform towards Bourne West Junction on 4th October 1958 revealed a fine collection of railway furniture including gas lamps, a water column with stove, and the inevitable telegraph poles. Great Northern lattice signal posts also survived, although following the withdrawal of Essendine passenger services in 1951 the branch was denied access from the platform roads and the relevant semaphore arm was removed. Photograph Barry Hilton.

Well after the Midland became part of the LMS and the Great Northern was absorbed by the LNER, Bourne still had a strong joint line identity. M&GN 0-6-0 No.69 stood at the station with an eastbound excursion in 1934. Despite its bucket of a chimney, the engine was thoroughbred Midland, whilst the coaches and platform canopy were clearly Great Northern. Photograph courtesy Vic Forster.

Ex-Great Northern class C12 4-4-2 tank No.4509 was shunting the sidings at the back of the goods yard on 23rd May 1931. It was relatively new to Lincolnshire and on this particular day had probably arrived on a goods working from Essendine. The tall yard lamps with their arm-like ladder supports were characteristic of Bourne. Photograph V.R. Webster.

Trains between Bourne and Spalding travelled across typical Fen country. Perfectly level ground stretches away as far as the eye can see, drainage channels abound, and straight roads connect the even scattering of brick farmhouses. Conditions could be very harsh – for instance from October 1880 to February 1881 the line was under 5ft of floodwater near Counter Drain. Class J6 0-6-0 No.64171 had a dry passage however as it approached Twenty with the 1.09 pm for Bourne on 5th July 1958. Photograph John Bonser.

North of Bourne a string of ten villages occupy the lower slopes of the limestone hills and when their parishes were extended to take in reclaimed fenland many of them grew large and prosperous. Indeed Billingborough was the size of many market towns when the Bourne – Sleaford branch opened. Unfortunately there were only three stations and bus services proved more convenient; thus the early demise of passenger services. Rippingale station, seen on 9th July 1959, featured steeply pitched roofs, scalloped bargeboards, slender finials and delightful little entrance porches, and was a forerunner of the bulky red brick structures characteristic of the GN's middle years. Goods services ceased in June 1964. Photograph John Bonser.

The Bourne to Saxby extension crossed the grain of the country and was the most heavily engineered section of the route from Norfolk to the Midlands. A 1 in 100 gradient took the railway up to Toft tunnel and beyond Little Bytham, where the tracks crossed the Great Northern main line and officially became Midland Railway property, there was a 300ft climb with embankments, cuttings and fifty blue brick bridges. At Little Bytham on 18th September 1954 a couple of Ivatt class 4MT Moguls guided the Birmingham New Street – Cromer, Yarmouth and Lowestoft train towards the coast as an express was signalled on the main line. Photograph V.R. Webster.

Bourne

In order to avoid hilly country the Bourne & Essendine Railway followed a somewhat indirect course involving negligible gradients and only light earthworks, but at least it was able to serve the village of Thurlby in the process. Otherwise it passed through an area of scattered hamlets and even these were remote from the line. For a while at the end, the old articulated twin coach branch set E44141/2 was hauled by brand new Ivatt class 4MT 2-6-0s, as on 5th June 1951 when No.43061 approached Thurlby with the 9.35 am from Bourne to Essendine. Sadly the station dog would soon have no more trains to watch as this was the last but one Tuesday of services. Thurlby and nearby Braceborough Spa station (where invalids once alighted for the isolated bathing establishment nearby) were plain brick buildings given some individuality by unusual moulded brick eaves. Both still exist in modified form. Photograph Mick Black.

The area between Bourne and Spalding is virtually devoid of villages and the stations at Twenty, Counter Drain and North Drove all derived their names from adjacent watercourses – although the first is also a hamlet. The buildings themselves were exceedingly plain and not dissimilar to nearby cottages, as could be seen on 5th July 1958 when an ex-LMS 4F 0-6-0 rushed through North Drove with a returning holiday train from Yarmouth Beach to Leicester London Road. Photograph John Bonser.

The western part of the Boston, Sleaford & Midland Counties Railway from Barkston to Sleaford crossed Lincoln Heath by a succession of rock cuttings and sweeping curves through the Ancaster Gap. Although Ancaster itself – the site of the important Roman town of Cavsennae on Ermine Street – had a pleasant stone building, later stations at Rauceby and Honington were plain brick structures livened up with fancy bargeboards. The Lincoln line diverged at the latter and as this was often used as a diversionary route for the East Coast main line, a couple of miles of the Sleaford route saw some prestigious trains. Peppercorn Pacific No.60141 ABBOTSFORD took the Lincoln track at Honington with the northbound 'Queen of Scots Pullman' on 27th September 1953. Photograph J.P. Wilson.

Seaside excursions from the East Midlands paused at Sleaford for the engines to take on water. This was also an opportunity to rake the coal forward and the firemen of ex-Great Northern J6 0-6-0 No.3541 and D2 4-4-0 No.4326 were busy on top of their respective tenders. It was Easter Monday 1930, thus explaining the heavy train of articulated GN non-corridor stock. This rare view of holiday traffic at Sleaford in LNER days was taken from a small print, as the original negative was destroyed during the 1939/45 War. Photograph John Clay.

Handley's Monument

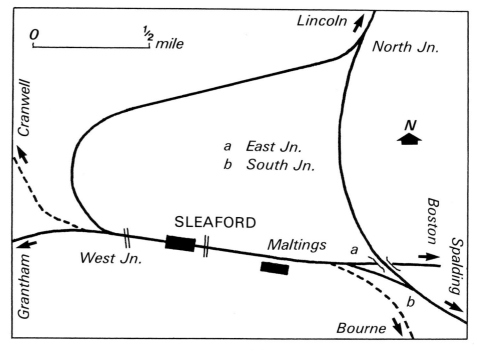

Of all Lincolnshire market towns, Sleaford probably sees the most holidaymakers, but they are passing through on their way to and from the coast, and relatively few people visit the focal point of north Kesteven for its own sake. Yet it is an attractive and in some ways surprising place, containing several remarkable buildings. Centuries ago it was described as 'truly melancholic' and the cathedral–like parish church dismissed as a 'cumbrous pile'. True, Sleaford did experience a slump in its fortunes, but once the River Slea was canalised in 1792 prosperity returned. The town was still flourishing when the railway arrived and it remains an important communications centre today, both in terms of its road links and, happily, its passenger train network.

In 1836 Sleaford lay on the route of an earlier proposed Great Northern Railway between London and York (not to be confused with its famous successor) but the scheme foundered. A decade later the Ambergate, Nottingham & Boston & Eastern Junction Railway also raised hopes in the town, but still no track materialised east of Grantham. However, Boston continued to press for a route to the Midlands and Sleaford was eager just to join in the Railway Age, so plans for the Bos-

ton, Sleaford & Midland Counties Railway were drawn up. This time all went well, and on 16th June 1857 an 11 mile branch from the GN main line north of Grantham, to Sleaford, opened for passenger traffic, followed by the 16¾ mile link to Boston on 12th April 1859. The line was single track throughout and was worked by the GN for 50% of the gross revenue. Before long the Great Eastern Railway was expressing interest in having its own route through Lincolnshire. Fearful of consequent traffic losses, the GN absorbed the BS & MC on 1st January 1865 and opened the Sleaford – Bourne line on 2nd January 1872 as part of a package of defensive measures. Never-

theless the GE arrived at Sleaford on 6th March 1882 via the GN/GE Joint line which passed ¾ of a mile east of the town and gained access to the existing station by means of connecting spurs. Unknown to the BS & MC promoters back in the 1850s, their line was destined to carry thousands of holidaymakers to Lincolnshire seaside resorts each year, and its doubling in 1877–81 reflected the sudden growth of this traffic. In the days of non–corridor stock the stop provided welcome relief for passengers as well, and the station facilities were notoriously inadequate!

Sleaford expanded considerably in Victorian

Sleaford also had long distance trains via the Joint Line. On 17th March 1956 B1 No.61311 departed with a York – Lowestoft train consisting of no less than 13 coaches of Gresley, Thompson and BR standard design. Photograph J.F. Henton.

times, notably west of the station where several streets of terraced houses provided working--class accommodation. Some substantial buildings appeared as well, and the town was particularly fortunate in having Kirk & Parry as its local architects. The firm was responsible for the stations of character on the Grantham – Lincoln line, and when it came to prestigious contracts in Sleaford they excelled themselves. Westholme House resembles a miniature chateau, whilst entrance lodges at the cemetery and gasworks were unashamedly Gothic fantasies. The use of Ancaster stone allowed them to blend well with the old town. Railways also strengthened Sleaford's role as an agricultural centre, as demonstrated by the establishment of a weekly livestock market in 1868. This relationship was emphasised in a truly spectacular way with the erection of a huge Bass malthouse complex east of the station during 1892-1905.

Passenger services on the 5¼ mile branch to Cranwell RAF College (which had opened in 1916) ceased in 1927, followed by those to Bourne on 22nd September 1930. But otherwise Sleaford's rail links remained intact – even through the Beeching years. Indeed, the Lincoln – Boston and Lincoln – Skegness services which had previously used other routes were diverted through the town in 1963 and 1970 respectively.

By August 1981 there was single track working towards Boston as far as Heckington as well as on the two links with the Joint line, but Sleaford's overall railway layout remained more or less as built. Although the direct Joint line route (or Sleaford avoiding line) had been under threat, it carried 17 freight and parcels trains daily in 1983 and was still available for East Coast main line Sunday diversions in 1992. Sleaford's passenger service is now considerably better than it was a quarter of a century ago – in fact there are nearly twice as many trains on weekdays. Although through carriages to Liverpool, Newcastle and Harwich are no more, there were 16 services to Boston or Skegness, 14 to Grantham and beyond, and 11 to Lincoln in 1991, compared with 9, 9 and 4 respectively in 1961. Sleaford station itself retains a lot of GN atmosphere: the original BS & MC building is a pleasant Tudor design in Ancaster stone, whilst the brick extensions, timber waiting room and platform canopies date from the opening of the Joint line in 1882. Unfortunately the original stone chimneys have recently been demolished, but generally the station is well looked after, and there is even a garden and ornamental pool. Until recently the nearby UKF depot received fertiliser from Ince in Lancashire by Railfreight, although the impressive maltings have been largely deserted.

East of Sleaford the Grantham – Boston line runs across the Fens and spends a lot of time sandwiched between South Forty Foot Drain and the A1121 road. Heckington and Swineshead stations date from the 1859 extension to Boston. The former is a large, rather ugly building with twin gable ends facing the platform and it provides a sharp contrast with the unique eight sail windmill of 1830 nearby and the richly decorated parish church half a mile away. Swineshead was similar, but in this view it was hidden by class B12/3 4-6-0 No.61538 picking a way through the clutter left by permanent way engineers during an all-stations Boston – Grantham working in June 1952. Photograph Les Perrin.

From 1971 all seasonal Skegness trains had to pass through Sleaford whether they originated in the East Midlands, Yorkshire or London. It was a bright start to the holiday for the southerners and Sleaford station looked as smart as ever as Brush Type 2 diesels 31209 and 31222 waited to leave for the seaside with the 09.25 King's Cross to Skegness on Saturday 10th August 1974. Photograph G.B. Wise.

Class 114 diesel railcars 53030 and 54011, which spent most of their 35 year life serving Lincolnshire but were at the time based at Birmingham's Tyseley depot, idled away part of Sunday afternoon at one of their old haunts on 15th May 1988. Much of the Great Northern atmosphere remains at Sleaford – indeed the line itself is remarkable in that Ancaster, Rauceby and Heckington still have GN station nameboards.

The true Great Eastern triumph as far as the Joint Line was concerned, was its vastly increased share of coal traffic. Holden 0-6-0 No.1181 (later class J17) headed south through Pinchbeck with a fully laden mineral train in the early 1900s. Stations on the Joint Line were particularly spacious. Photograph courtesy of Les Prudden.

K3 2-6-0 No.61873 of March shed (31B) steamed through Pinchbeck with a mixed freight for Whitemoor yards on 11th July 1951. The station was beginning to shows its age, having already lost its platform canopy and a few finials. It has now been demolished. Photograph J.P. Wilson.

Having closed to passengers on 11th September 1961 and goods on 7th September 1964, Ruskington station was allowed to become very derelict. Brush Type 2 diesel No.31103 headed north past the wilderness with a freight consisting largely of metal scrap on 12th August 1974. Of the original Joint Line station buildings, only Gosberton and Digby survived by the late 1980s. Photograph G.B. Wise.

Chapter 10
The Joint Line

Dunston Pillar

Alongside the Sleaford road six miles south of Lincoln stands Dunston Pillar. Of all things, this was once a lighthouse to guide travellers across the vast expanse of furze and bracken which made up Lincoln Heath. Eventually the wetlands were improved, and nowadays the fields of beet and barley are a far cry from the inhospitable scene of two centuries ago. Eastwards towards the Witham valley the wilderness gave way to more fertile land which supported several large villages such as Metheringham and Ruskington. Many of them gained a station in 1882 – but this was incidental, for the railway which skirted the Heath was born of grand territorial ambitions rather than a desire to be of service locally.

The origins of the line go back to the heady 1840s when the Eastern Counties Railway, under the dynamic leadership of George Hudson, had visions of itself as a trunk route from London to

the north. Completion of the Great Northern effectively shattered this dream and condemned the East Anglian concern to an impoverished, agricultural existence. This was made all the more frustrating by the mere trickle of lucrative Yorkshire – London coal traffic it was able to carry. Sheer weakness forced the EC to tolerate this situation, but in 1862 it became the core of the new Great Eastern Railway which saw an extension northwards as its only salvation. A series of revolutions in the GE boardroom hindered progress, but the GN nevertheless endeavoured to protect its territory by promoting new lines such as Bourne to Sleaford and Spalding to March. Eventually, after a plethora of rival schemes and near merger, the GN and GE reached a compromise in the form of the Great Northern & Great Eastern Joint Railway.

On 1st August 1882 the 37½ mile Lincoln – Sleaford – Spalding line became fully operational and the Joint Committee assumed responsibility for a 120 mile loop from Doncaster to Huntingdon, the balance being made up of existing GN and GE tracks. South of Sleaford the new line ran largely across the Fens, with long straight level sections and some twenty level crossings. Large goods sheds were provided for dealing with the prolific agricultural produce, notably beet and potatoes. North of Sleaford, where the route kept to the eastern flank of the Heath, there were more overbridges and earthworks – notably the rock cuttings at Nocton and Washingborough. Over this section the gradients were carefully arranged to favour loaded southbound freights. Ironically the Joint line actually hurt the GN. Its value as relief for the congested main line was less than expected, and the GE soon became established as a major competitor. Doncaster – London Liverpool Street trains commenced and boat trains from Lancashire to Harwich soon followed. Eventually long–distance services from Liverpool, York and Newcastle to Ipswich, Norwich and Yarmouth put Lincolnshire on an entirely new traffic artery.

Leaving aside individual company fortunes, the general concept of the Joint line as an alternative to the GN's overcrowded main line and its circuitous loop through Boston was well founded. Impressive GE 4–4–0s and 4–6–0s became a familiar sight on passenger trains, and the LNER 'Sandringham' B17 4–6–0s built as replacements remained until the advent of diesel traction. Through goods traffic was consistently heavy, especially after the Whitemoor Marshalling Yard at March was commissioned in 1928.

The GE even managed to stamp its personality on Lincolnshire architecturally, for the eleven local stations were typical of the company's contemporary style. They consisted of twin–pavilion single-storey red brick buildings with decorative work in cream brick, ornate bargeboards and large platform canopies. Station houses were substantial but more subdued and crossing cottages were decidedly plain. Several remote country stations closed in 1955 – Scopwick & Timberland (1¾ miles from either village) for instance. The remainder succomed on 11th September 1961 along with the Doncaster – March stopping service.

Its importance as a major ingress to East Anglia meant that the line survived Beeching unscathed, and in the early 1970s descendants of the *North Country Continental* boat trains still rolled steadily along the edge of the Heath past the decaying remains of once–proud GE stations. However, changes were imminent. On 7th May 1973 the Harwich service was diverted via Nottingham, Grantham and Peterborough leaving regular passenger workings solely in the hands of DMU's. Locomotive hauled seasonal holiday trains from northern England to Skegness and Great Yarmouth continued however. Freight traffic was also winding down, and the big 9F 2–10–0s and WD 2–8–0s of the 1950s had been replaced by diesels. But after nearly 14 years without trains Ruskington believed it deserved them once more, so with Lincolnshire County Council supported a new halt opened on 5th May 1975. Metheringham joined in the revival on 6th October 1975.

On 1st November 1982 the century–old role of the Joint line as a route between East Anglia and the north came to an end with closure of the Spalding – March section. Fortunately the Spalding – Peterborough line remained as a southern outlet – but only as a result of local authority rescue following the East Lincolnshire closures of October 1970. Nowadays, the GN/GE route remains double track, looks as prosperous as ever, and is available for East Coast main line engineering diversions. In 1992 the first generation railcars finally retired from the line and were replaced by Sprinters, including the new single car class 153 units. Although there were just four services each way between Sleaford and Spalding on weekdays, the Lincoln – Sleaford section had 15 southbound and 14 northbound – a far superior service to that of 1961. At the same time plans were announced for new stations at Donington and Pinchbeck.

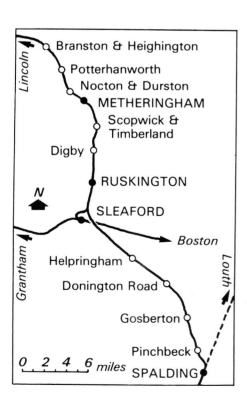

Branston & Heighington
Potterhanworth
Nocton & Durston
METHERINGHAM
Scopwick & Timberland
Digby
RUSKINGTON
SLEAFORD
Boston
Helpringham
Donington Road
Gosberton
Pinchbeck
SPALDING
Lincoln
Grantham
Louth
N
0 2 4 6 miles

On Saturday 26th July 1975, EE Type 4 No.40012 AUREOL roared through the reopened Ruskington station with the 13.22 Skegness – Manchester Piccadilly. Photograph G.B. Wise.

37

The former Joint Line nature of Spalding persisted in BR days. Ex-Great Northern class J6 0-6-0 No.64260 hauling three LMS coaches formed a local M&GN line train one winter morning in the mid 1950s. Ivatt 4MT 2-6-0 No.43065 also an M&GN line engine, looked on from the outermost platform. Photograph courtesy Neville Stead.

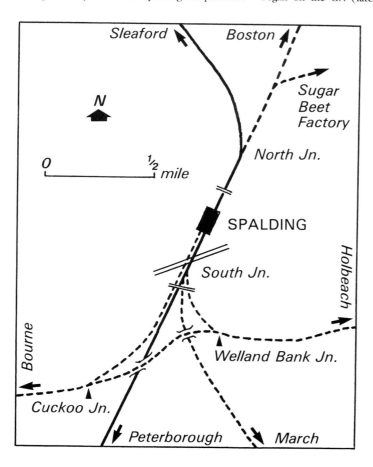

Tulip Fields

Chapter 11
Spalding

As the lowest bridging point on the River Welland and the limit of navigation for sea–going ships, Spalding became a flourishing trading centre in medieval times. Ayscoughfee Hall and the parish church are worthy reminders of that prosperity. Affluence returned in the 1700s when there were numerous agricultural fairs and the quays bustled with the transhipment of coal, timber, cornflour and Fenland produce. Handsome warehouses and fine dwellings were built alongside the Welland and the antiquarian 'Gentlemen's Society of Spalding' came into being. Railways sustained Spalding's importance

in Victorian times, especially after it became the intersection of three main lines. Much rebuilding took place and the town lost some of its 18th century appearance, through certainly not its character. In marked contrast, Crowland, just 8 miles away, remained virtually unchanged – largely as a result of its isolation from the railway system.

Early plans for railways in south Lincolnshire largely revolved around the conflict between George Hudson and the Great Northern. After all the wrangling, it was the GN which provided Spalding with its first station when the Peterborough – Lincoln 'loop' opened on 17th October 1848. Furthermore, the company was involved in one way or another with every railway development affecting Spalding over the next half century. Few small towns enjoyed such a relentless growth of new railway routes. On 15th November 1858 GN passenger trains began to run to Holbeach over the locally promoted Norwich & Spalding Railway, which hoped to extend its 7½ miles of track into Norfolk when cash became available. 1st August 1866 saw the first workings between Spalding and Bourne, whilst on 2nd September 1867 passenger services began on the GN (later GN/GE Joint) line to

March, built to counter the Great Eastern's ambitions. When the GE got its own way in the form of the Joint line, Spalding gained yet another outlet – this time to Sleaford on 6th March 1882. Finally, on 1st May 1894 the newly formed Midland & Great Northern Joint Committee opened its Spalding avoiding line. For a sumptuous but all too brief period, Spalding saw locomotives adorned in the GN's bright green, the rich blue of the GE, the Midland's glowing crimson and the distinctive yellow ochre of the M & GN.

Originally Spalding station consisted of two platforms, a small amenities building and a three storey house, but the opening of new routes – especially the GN/GE Joint line – demanded a substantial increase in facilities. The final layout comprised two large islands as well as the main platform, together with a couple of bays. With the use of yellow brick and some round headed windows, additional buildings were generally in harmony with the original design. Extensive goods yards were also necessary. Around 1900 the Spalding area became noted for potato growing, whilst Holbeach was a major centre for soft fruits, and distribution was almost entirely by rail.

For many years road competition hardly

Brush Type 4s 47020, 47111, 47072, 47566 and EE Type 3 37035 brought Flower Parade specials from Swansea, Bristol, Oxford, Portsmouth and Wokingham respectively on 10th May 1980. Photograph G.B. Wise.

South of Spalding station the lines to Holbeach, March, Peterborough and Bourne diverged and there was a huge acreage of railway land which effectively prevented the town from growing in this direction. An exceptionally long metal footbridge crossed all four sets of tracks as can be seen in this 25th August 1964 view, but by this time the avoiding line girders beyond it had been dismantled. Photograph John Bonser.

affected Spalding's railways. Even when lorries had poached much general agricultural traffic, a big sugar beet factory was opened near the Boston line in 1926 and bulk loads of beet were delivered by rail. All six routes were served by stopping trains and long distance expresses as late as 1958, but the rot started with the withdrawal of M & GN line passenger services on 28th February 1959. The former M & GN lines remained open for freight until 1965 when they became victims of Beeching's recommendation that uneconomic goods traffic should be abandoned. A much more serious outcome of his report, albeit somewhat belated, was closure of the Grimsby – Peterborough route, resulting in the end of Grimsby – King's Cross expresses via Spalding on 3rd October 1970. With financial support from Spalding and Holland councils, the Spalding – Peterborough section was re opened

with a basic service on 7th June 1971. Diversion of the Harwich boat trains on 7th May 1973 meant the end of regular main line workings through Spalding, and the town was left with just DMU's.

During May Spalding comes alive with its annual flower parade. Rather than an ancient pagan ritual, this ceremony is an enterprising way of using the waste product of the tulip industry, and began as recently as 1959. In order to promote sturdy bulbs the flowers are cut off, and until they were used with considerable flair to decorate floats, the heads lay in colourful but largely unseen carpets in farmyards. For a short but fascinating period, BR exploited the excursion potential that this spectacle offered. In 1980 for instance, specials brought day trippers from Bristol, Cardiff, Chorley, Congleton, Coventry, Hull, King's Cross, Manchester, Moreton–in–

Marsh, Newcastle, Oxford, Plymouth, Portsmouth, Runcorn, Shenfield, Stroud, Swansea, Weston–super–Mare and Wokingham.

Despite this burst of activity rationalisation had not yet finished at Spalding. Traffic to the sugar factory ceased in 1980, most of the goods yards were removed, and after the customary TUCC enquiry trains to March ceased on 1st November 1982. Further track recovery left just two through lines and a handful of sidings from 28th July 1984. With its six routes and through expresses merely memories, the station is now a ghost of its former self. Nevertheless, the Peterborough service has enjoyed a substantial increase in patronage over recent years, a £3 million cash injection for the Peterborough–Doncaster line has recently been announced, and there were even a couple of specials to the flower festival in 1992.

The East Anglian flavour at Spalding also extended well into the BR era. March based class B17/6 4-6-0 No.61633 KIMBOLTON CASTLE was a glorious sight in late afternoon sunshine after a sweltering day as it drew away with the Liverpool Central – Harwich Parkeston Quay boat train on 24th July 1952. These engines were specially designed by Gresley for the former Great Eastern lines of the LNER. Photograph J. Cupit.

Just over a year earlier, on 7th July 1951, B17/6 No.61635 MILTON was in charge of the Liverpool – Harwich boat train. This time the weather was overcast, but if anything the loco was in even better external condition. Photograph J.P. Wilson.

The original Great Northern route through Spalding also had its expresses. On 16th April 1947 ex-Great Central class B3 4-6-0 No.1494 LORD FARINGDON called with the morning train from Cleethorpes and Grimsby to London King's Cross. Photograph H.C. Casserley.

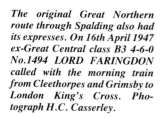

Besides long-distance trains, Spalding had numerous all-stations locals which were once important to isolated Fenland communities. In the early 1930s ex-Great Eastern 'Claud Hamilton' 4-4-0 No.8861 waited to leave for Cowbit, Postland, French Drive and March whilst an M&GN 0-6-0 at the far platform was probably heading for North Drove, Counter Drain, Twenty and Bourne. Photograph Courtesy D.L. Franks.

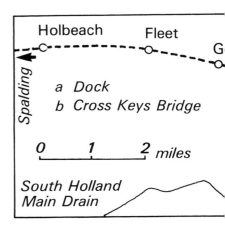

A low ridge of silt stretches from Spalding through Holbeach towards Norfolk. Before extensive reclamation work it provided a refuge between 'foul woosy marsh' bordering the Wash and 'foggy fens' with 'vast and queachy soil' to the south, according to one writer. In fact the ridge has long been settled and its past prosperity resulted in some of the most magnificent parish churches in England, as at Long Sutton, Gedney and Fleet. However, crossing the River Nene east of Long Sutton was a dangerous business and wise travellers employed a guide – after all, King John of Magna Carta fame lost his jewels during one attempt!

In 1831 a timber bridge was built across the Nene and Long Sutton prospered. Furthermore, a new township called Sutton Bridge developed, and its wharves and warehouses soon had a flourishing trade in timber, coal and corn. Although the bridge was an outstanding engineering feat for the time, it was replaced in 1850 by an iron swingbridge designed by Robert Stephenson.

Railway development in the south east corner of Lincolnshire was piecemeal, complex and very colourful. The Norwich & Spalding Railway, having reached Holbeach from Spalding in 1858, mustered enough funds to extend to Sutton Bridge on 1st July 1862. Next came the Lynn & Sutton Bridge Railway which, in the pursuit of economy, purchased the 1850 bridge and adapted the structure for both road and rail traffic. Its trains began to run into a separate Sutton Bridge station on 1st March 1866. Finally the Peterborough, Wisbech & Sutton Bridge Railway, worked by the Midland rather than the GN, opened on 1st August 1866. Within a short time the entire 37 mile Bourne – Spalding – King's

Lynn line had become the Midland & Eastern Railway, operated jointly by the GN and Midland. The next twist to the story came on 1st.July 1883 when the M&E and PW&SB became part of the Eastern & Midlands Railway which had been formed from certain local Norfolk lines six months earlier. One of its constituents, the Lynn & Fakenham Railway, had just taken delivery of four Beyer Peacock 4–4–0s and by 1888 these handsome engines, in a chocolate livery lined out in red, white and blue, were working newly–introduced Cromer – King's Cross expresses as far as Peterborough. But the E&M sunk into a chronic financial state and the Midland & Great Northern Joint Committee took it over completely on 1st. July 1893. Engines characteristic of the parent companies but resplendent in the new M&GN golden ochre livery soon began to appear.

There was a time when the GN wanted to forget Sutton Bridge. It had contributed £55,000 towards construction costs of the new dock there, and when *The Garland* sailed with a cargo of Derbyshire coal on 14th May 1881 there was deep satisfaction about the promising export business ahead. But within days the lock gate foundations had collapsed and some facing wall had fallen, so the 13 acre basin, together with the latest in hydraulic machinery, proved totally useless – and remained so. Shortly afterwards the Great Eastern was happily plundering GN territory by means of the Joint line, so King's Cross renewed its interest in the railway penetrating deep into Norfolk. Once the M&GN had been formed, GN directors were quite happy to share the £80,000 cost of the new Cross Keys swing bridge at Sutton Bridge. This impressive steel structure, which had a 176ft swinging span, came

into operation on 18th July 1897 and within a few years up to 80 trains a day were using it.

Norfolk coast holiday traffic, fish from Lowestoft and manufactured goods from Norwich continued to flow along the lengthy single track through south Lincolnshire after the M & GN became LMS/LNER Joint in 1923, but there were

Holbeach   Fleet   G

Spalding

a Dock
b Cross Keys Bridge

0   1   2 miles

South Holland
Main Drain

The M&GN inherited a wide variety of station architecture from its assorted constituents. Both stages of the Norwich & Spalding had a distinctive style. Tall gaunt buildings with half-hearted decorative work and a curious gable end chimney set at an angle were found on the 1858 line, as can still be seen at Moulton and Holbeach, whilst the Sutton Bridge extension had lower, more pleasing, stations with lean-to apron roofs between end blocks, as at Fleet and Gedney which still survive. Tydd in its exposed Fenland setting, was typical of the unimaginative affairs put up by the PW&SB. Melton Constable based Ivatt 2-6-0 No.43156 left Tydd with the 12.42 pm Yarmouth Beach – Peterborough North on 4th October 1958. Photograph Barry Hilton.

ridge

The 1831 Bridge

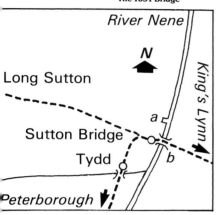

ominous signs. As the proud yellow ochre livery disappeared, increasing numbers of lorries and charabancs crossed the road part of Cross Keys bridge and there was a marked decline in the amount of cattle and general agricultural products carried. At least the new seaside holiday camps of the 1930s kept the 'Leicesters' busy during summer. In 1936 the LNER took over the system and shortly afterwards most of the remaining M&GN engines were scrapped. The new Ivatt Moguls allocated to the line in the early 1950s ushered in a new era, but this proved to be short lived.

By the mid–1950s the M&GN had lost most of its freight, with the notable exception of sugar beet, taken to factories in bulk loads. Yet this was only a seasonal operation, as was the still–substantial holiday traffic. BR was in serious financial difficulties and this particular line lost money heavily, so its fate was sealed. Thankfully there was no undignified run down and a full service was maintained until the end, which came on Saturday 28th February 1959. It was by far the largest single closure seen on Britain's railways, for 24 stations and over 160 miles of

passenger route from Leicestershire and Peterborough to Norwich and the Norfolk coast perished on that day. Cross Keys bridge was converted to two way road traffic in 1960 and a goods branch was maintained from Spalding to Sutton Bridge until 1965.

There are several reminders of the M&GN and its predecessors. The two stages of the Norwich and Spalding were clearly distinguished by station styling, and a couple of good examples of each survive. Tall, gaunt buildings with half hearted decorative work and a curious gable end chimney set at an angle were found on the 1858 line, as can be seen at Moulton and Holbeach. The Sutton Bridge extension had lower, more pleasing stations with lean to apron roofs between end blocks, as at Fleet and Gedney. Tydd, in its exposed Fenland setting, is typical of the unimaginative affairs put up by the PW & SB. By 1988 Sutton Bridge bypass was nearing completion but local protests in addition to financial considerations led to the decision to retain Cross Keys bridge rather than build a new swingbridge. So the distinctive M&GN structure is secure for the foreseeable future.

An early decision of the M&GN Joint Committee was to spend £80,000 on a new Cross Keys swingbridge at Sutton Bridge. This impressive steel structure, which had a 176ft swinging span, came into operation on 18th July 1897 and within a few years 80 trains a day were using it. Seen from the train, an ex-Great Eastern class D16/3 4-4-0 with LMS coaches headed east across the bridge towards Norfolk. Photograph V.R. Webster.

On a grim winter day gritting lorries going over Cross Keys bridge passed Ivatt 2-6-0 No.43092 of 31D South Lynn shed, arriving at Sutton Bridge with a westbound local. In reality it was the trains that were going – for good. Saturday 28th February 1959 saw the end of 24 stations and 160 passenger route miles from Saxby and Peterborough to Norwich and Yarmouth. Cross Keys bridge was converted to two-way road traffic in 1960 and is still a prominent feature of the town. Photograph F.E. Quenby.

Immingham B1s usually handled Grimsby – King's Cross expresses in the 1950s and latterly they worked all the way to London rather than being replaced at Peterborough. With safety valves blowing, No.61379 MAYFLOWER stood amid the magnificent array of signals at the south end of Boston station on 16th April 1958, as it prepared to journey south. Photograph Les Perrin.

Chapter 13
Boston

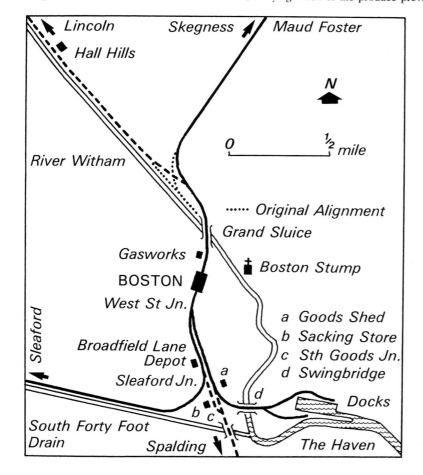

Boston Stump

In AD 654 St. Botolph founded a monastery near the mouth of the River Witham and eventually a small settlement grew up nearby, principally because the estuary provided a safe haven for boats. Five centuries later Boston was a medieval boom town with a port second only to London in the volume of trade handled. Its annual fair attracted people from all over England, and even Europe. A spectacular celebration of this affluence was the mighty parish church of St. Botolph – Boston Stump – which has long been one of Lincolnshire's greatest landmarks. In 1607 the Pilgrim Fathers fled from Boston in an unsuccessful attempt to escape religious persecution. They were captured and imprisoned in the Guildhall, but their famous voyage from Southampton aboard the *Mayflower* came 13 years later. In 1630 another band of Puritans set sail from Lincolnshire and founded Boston, Massachusetts. Water transport continued to dominate the town. Apart from coastal and continental shipping, the harbour served numerous packet boats plying the Fenland waterways. Grand Sluice, which separated the River Witham from the tidal channel of The Haven was completed in 1766 and for a while Boston actually had a slightly higher population than Lincoln itself.

With the spread of railways during the 1840s Boston naturally wished to protect and ideally expand its port facilities. So the town reacted favourably to proposals for lines from Nottingham and Birmingham which promised to bring coal and manufactured goods for shipment. A Midlands connection failed to materialise at first and instead Boston became an intermediate station on the Great Northern's Peterborough – Lincoln 'loop' line as well as the junction for the East Lincolnshire Railway to Grimsby – both of them north–south routes. The latter was completed on 2nd October 1848 and the opening of the 'loop' fifteen days later was celebrated by a sumptuous banquet laid on by the Mayor and Corporation for GN directors and other worthies. Initially the harbour had gained extra business by unloading pig iron and timber for construction work, but before long the trains were carrying much of the produce previously handled by coasters and decline was inevitable. The town acquired its much–desired link with the Midlands on 12th April 1859 when the Boston, Sleaford & Midland Counties Railway was finally made ready throughout. Originally it was planned to terminate this line at a substantial new docks complex – the decision to join the 'loop' at Sleaford Junction instead was indicative of Boston's changing transport pattern.

Following its brief spell of glory from August 1850 to August 1852 when all GN trains between London and the North called at Boston, the station assumed a more modest role as the hub of local services in east Lincolnshire. It still had its Grimsby – King's Cross through trains and these were often hauled by the latest main line motive power. Otherwise this particular part of the GN system became a haven for engines in their twilight years.

The railway occupied a broad sweep of land on the western side of Boston and contributed a considerable amount of interest to the local urban landscape. Three substantial bridges were required: across South Forty Foot Drain, at Grand Sluice and over Maud Foster Drain. A temporary station had to suffice at first and when the permanent structure opened in November 1850 it was a rather disappointing effort with far less character than supposedly less important buildings elsewhere on the 'loop'. The platforms were widely separated to accommodate four through lines and each had a canopy extending over the nearest track – no doubt GN frugality ruled out an overall roof! The undistinguished frontage had a projecting arcade, but even this was disfigured during alterations in 1911, resulting in the present untidy appearance.

South of the station there were numerous properties associated with the railway. A massive grain warehouse was erected next to the South Forty Foot Drain in 1848 to intercept water–borne traffic and divert it from the docks to the GN. A couple of mills were rail-served, including Cooper & Son's granary with its elegantly–curved wall following the line of a siding. Railway premises included the sacking store, goods depots, engineers' yards and the original locomotive works and engine shed. The extensive Hall Hills sleeper depot was constructed alongside the Lincoln line in 1904.

Although Boston docks suffered with the arrival of the GN, the town grew suddenly with the influx of railway workers and their families. In the decade up to 1851 the population increased by 20% and the company became the largest single employer of local labour. Housing development had to keep pace. By 1848 King Street and Duke Street had been crammed into the restricted space between the existing town and the railway. Station Street was thrust across the fields towards the station itself and incorporated the 'Great Northern' hostelry. Station Street survives more or less in its original form, and Duke Street is still there – albeit with many cottages now replaced by modern houses.

Boston's railway layout underwent several changes over the years. Just nine months after the first passenger train, approval was sought for an alteration to the northern approach which suffered from a single track section squeezed between the grounds of a large house and the River Witham. This led to an awkward, sharply curved approach to Grand Sluice bridge which had to be negotiated by both GN and EL trains. The new line opened on 12th May 1850. South of the station the volume of traffic justified the opening of separate passenger lines from West Street Junction to South Goods Junction in November 1875, leaving the original lines for freight, and in May 1879 the BS & MC line from Hubbert's Bridge to Sleaford Junction was doubled.

During the 1880s Boston was revitalised as a port. There had been proposals to construct a harbour by the shore of the Wash near Freiston; instead the Haven was improved and the Boston Docks & Harbour Commission went ahead with a new basin close to the town centre. By early 1885 the facilities were nearing completion and over the next few years there was a considerable growth in trade – coal exports and timber imports especially – thanks mainly to the larger vessels which could be handled. A new branch served the dock estate via a swingbridge over the Haven, but otherwise the GN was unwilling to become involved in maritime activities after the fiasco at Sutton Bridge. Meanwhile the timber viaduct at Grand Sluice was in need of renewal, and its 1885 replacement has been one of the better known features of Boston's railway scene for over a century.

As early as February 1848 the GN decided to build locomotive and rolling stock workshops at Boston, although these were not completed until several months after the loop line opened. A substantial and dignified office block marked the entrance to the site in Broadfield Lane. At one stage it seemed likely that the works would actually expand, but Boston was not destined to become a major railway town. By mid-1853 the mighty Doncaster plant was firmly established and most of the Lincolnshire workforce had been transferred there. Broadfield Lane continued to function as an engine shed providing power for local passenger, goods, and shunting duties – with some locomotive repairs undertaken as well.

Although remote from the East Coast main line, Boston remained a busy railway centre in the 1950s. There were trip workings to and from the docks; local stations over a wide area were served by daily pick–up goods trains; the yard received and dispatched long–distance goods traffic; and through freight included express fish from Grimsby and iron ore for Scunthorpe. During the summer season, numerous holiday trains to and from Skegness and Mablethorpe were scheduled between the local passenger services. The 1960s were not happy times through, for Beeching saw Boston's future role as a minor terminus at the end of a branch from Grantham. The Lincoln service succumbed on 17th June 1963, Broadfield Lane depot closed in January 1964 and goods traffic dwindled rapidly. An eruption of protests saved the Grimsby line and the remainder of the loop for a while, but from 5th October 1970 Boston did, indeed, become the railhead for much of east Lincolnshire.

The last twenty years have seen a heavy toll on Boston's railway infrastructure, yet there is still tantalising evidence of busier days and the GN still seems to have an indefinable presence. A broad sweep of past and present railway land continues to dominate the western flank of the town and much of it stands as waste ground or has experienced piecemeal redevelopment, although a fragment carries running lines and sidings. One by one, many familiar features disappeared. The signal boxes at Sleaford Junc-

Houses in Duke Street built for the influx of railway workers a century earlier formed the background as K3 2-6-0 No.61905 took the Grantham line at Sleaford Junction with a Skegness – Birmingham New Street return excursion on 12th June 1948. The train was about to pass the crossing and footbridge leading to Locomotive Street and the engine sheds. Photograph J.P. Wilson.

tion, Wyberton Road, Maud Foster and Grand Sluice were taken out of commission and demolished between 1974 and 1987. Broadfield Lane depot, its coaling tower, the engineers' yard and one of the goods sheds suffered a similar fate. The huge granary expired in a spectacular way. It was being used for storing wood shavings when boys up to mischief started a blaze on 13th October 1985. Firemen commented on how well the massive walls had stood up to the inferno.

Boston itself remains a busy market centre and attracts many tourists, including Americans investigating their ancestry. The town also has ghosts other than those of the railway. Prominent from the station is an ornate Victorian building surmounted by a carved swan – a former feather factory harking back to the days of eiderdowns and feather pillows. Fishing boats still berth at the Haven quays and the docks are busy with timber and agricultural merchandise. Some grain and imported steel is handled by rail, requiring the Dock Authority's class 08 shunter to rumble over the swingbridge past the delightful little control cabin.

B1 No.1175, just a year old and resplendent in apple green, passed Maud Foster box on the outskirts of Boston with a Lincoln Central – Skegness local via Sleaford and Boston on 12th June 1948. The neat crossing house with its low pitched roof and distinctive windows was typical of East Lincolnshire Railway practice. Photograph J.P. Wilson.

The River Witham and Great Northern Railway came together at Grand Sluice within sight of Boston Stump. A massive barrier of masonry and metalwork converted the Fenland drain into a tidal channel and this was overseen by the 1885 bowstring bridge spans. Class B17/6 4-6-0 No.61643 CHAMPION LODGE drifted across the girders with the 9.47 am Doncaster – March train on 6th June 1958. Photograph Les Perrin.

Seen from the footbridge to Locomotive Street, K3 2-6-0 No.61940 was making a determined departure from Boston with the morning Doncaster – March train on 12th May 1956. A freight is heading north past a J6 0-6-0 in Broadfield Lane sidings and rows of wagons await attention in the nearby workshops. Photograph Les Perrin.

With a full head of steam, class B1 4-6-0 No.61281 was ready for its 9.43 am departure from Woodhall Junction with a Lincoln Central to Skegness working on 29th April 1954. The station nameboard invited passengers to explore places further east and the gents' urinal survived as a gem of Victoriana. Photograph R.M. Casserley.

Algarkirk & Sutterton station between Boston and Spalding – seen here in 1950 – was one of the more conventional buildings on the 'loop' and featured a pitched roof with large overhangs. It closed on 11th September 1961 and is now a private residence. The importance of agricultural traffic is shown by the two yards and large goods shed which remained open until June 1964.

Horncastle branch trains fed traffic into the 'loop' for nearly a century and they had their own platform at Woodhall Junction. Because the actual branch connection faced away from the station, coaches had to be propelled into the bay and class N5 0-6-2 tank No.69253 and its crew relaxed there following an afternoon journey from Horncastle on 7th April 1953. Photograph John Bonser.

Tattershall Castle

The River Witham drops just 12 ft. in the 36 miles from Lincoln to Boston Haven and in its natural shallow state, meandered along a marshy, flood–prone valley. Nevertheless this was an important trade route, and during the 1760s the waterway was straightened and made to run between artificial banks. Transformation of the surrounding area into fertile farmland soon followed, with wind and steam pumps constantly draining water from big 'delphs' fed by a network of ditches. A steam packet boat was introduced along the Witham between Lincoln and Boston in 1814, though the journey still took most of the day. Thirty years later travel between the two towns was about to undergo a revolution. There were several schemes for railways along the Witham valley and eventually one came to fruition. In 1846 the Great Northern purchased the Witham Navigation and construction of the 58 miles of Lincolnshire 'loop' line from Peterborough to Lincoln via Spalding and Boston commenced early in 1847. Much of the route

consisted of straight level sections and the only engineering works of note were 32 iron or timber bridges across waterways. The line opened on 17th October 1848.

From Boston to Lincoln most of the 'loop' was actually laid on the eastern bank of the Witham, but the river occasionally makes a sudden change of course as a result of the 18th century improvements, so trains had their otherwise steady progress impeded by a series of abrupt curves. Nine stations were provided on this section, mostly adjacent to traditional ferry crossings. Initially the loop had main line status and enjoyed royal patronage when Queen Victoria travelled this way to Balmoral in August 1851, but in 1852 most through traffic was taken away by the GN main line. The Horncastle Railway generated plenty of extra local business from 1855 and the Louth branch attempted to do the same in 1876. Kirkstead (eventually renamed Woodhall Junction) and Bardney stations were elevated to junction status and each gained an extra platform. Eventually the basic passenger service consisted of Lincoln – Boston and Lincoln – Skegness locals, the latter using the Kirkstead – Little Steeping line of 1913. Some Doncaster – March trains used the 'loop' in order to serve Boston, seaside excursions were frequent in summer, and anglers' specials from industrial towns called at every station alongside the Witham.

Coal traffic from Doncaster to London was a considerable source of revenue for the GN, and much of it went via the 'loop' rather than the main line. Delays to prestige expresses were thus avoided and the lack of gradients meant that engines could cope with half as many wagons again. Large 0–6–0s capable of hauling 700 ton trains entered service in the 1870s specifically for this purpose and five refuge sidings were installed between Lincoln and Boston at the same time, principally because of the sheer volume of coal being moved.

Although the GN/GE Joint line provided an alternative route between Lincoln and Spalding from 1882, diverted traffic often used the 'loop'

when the main line was unavailable. The section from Coningsby Junction (south of Woodhall Junction) to Boston, together with passenger and goods facilities at Tattershall, Dogdyke and Langrick, perished on 17th June 1963. Ironically, some Lincoln – Boston services via Sleaford were actually a few minutes faster than those they replaced on the direct line. The remainder of the 'loop' lost its passenger trains when the Lincoln – Skegness and Peterborough – Grimsby services were withdrawn in 1970, although the Spalding – Peterborough section was later reinstated. The Horncastle pick–up goods served Woodhall Junction until 6th April 1971 and seasonal trip workings, from Lincoln Holmes Yard to the sugar factory at Bardney, lasted until 1983. The closure saved the expense of maintaining Greetwell Junction signal box in Lincoln, but was much against British Sugar Corporation's wishes.

Nowadays much of the former trackbed alongside the river is little more than a grassy footpath, although several of the 'loop' line buildings survive as little islands of nostalgia. These early examples of GN architecture were curious – strange even. A square three–storey tower with a pyramidal roof and round headed windows was the main feature at Bardney, Woodhall Junction, Tattershall, Spalding and Peakirk, but there were delightful detail differences. Yellow bricks were used, except at Woodhall Junction where they merely provided relief to red brick. At Bardney and Woodhall Junction huge top–heavy and ornate chimneys rose above oddly chamfered roofs. Dogdyke, which opened in 1849, consisted of an apologetic version of the earlier towers and virtually nothing else. Nondescript red brick buildings were deemed adequate for lesser stations – but here was another anomaly. An indifferent half timbered cottage was provided at Deeping, despite the importance of the town as a stage coach stop and water transport centre when the railway arrived. Yet Langrick had a large building with a peculiar little pantiled belfry – something special amid the dull houses of a tiny Fenland village.

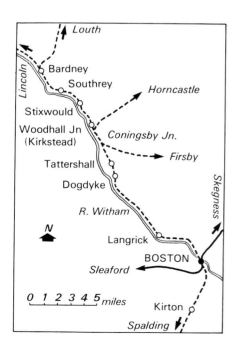

This view of Woodhall Junction on 21st September 1969 sums up the unique character of the Lincoln – Boston line. The three storey station house with its round headed windows and large chimneys was a prominent feature in the flat Fen landscape while the track itself followed the raised bank of the River Witham. Horncastle trains veered off to the left behind the goods yard. Originally there was a ferry at Kirkstead but eventually the Metheringham – Horncastle road became important enough to warrant a bridge and this was replaced by the present structure during the 1960s.

Chapter 14
The Loop

Both the agricultural nature of the area, represented by various tractors and trailers, and the optimism of the Horncastle Railway Company, demonstrated by the grand stone entrance, were apparent in this exterior view of Horncastle station on 21st September 1969. Goods facilities were withdrawn within 18 months but the Georgian terminus building – in sympathy with the town architecturally – survived for another 15 years.

Ex-Great Eastern Railway class N7 0-6-2 tank No.9672 taking a holiday from Liverpool Street suburban duties in London introduced the unfamiliar 'pish-tish' of its Westinghouse brake pump to Horncastle during 1948. Although the outsider soon returned south it looked quite at home on the branch service. Photograph T.G. Hepburn.

There were plenty of wagons at the goods dock and a string of coal trucks near the canal wharf on 12th June 1951 but very few passengers as class N5 0-6-2 tank No.69275 waited at Horncastle with the 4.05 pm for Woodhall Junction. The former Railway Hotel just to the right of the station nameboard was in the same style as the main building and still exists. Photograph Mick Black.

Chapter 15

Horncastle & Woodhall

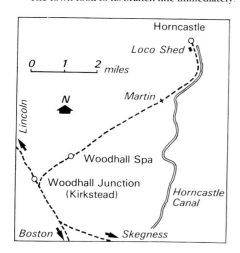

Ruins of Kirkstead Abbey

The area north of Tattershall was once a snake-infested heath where local lords and abbots did their hunting. Woodland thrived on the sandy soil but crops did not, so few people settled there. Beyond the heathland stood Horncastle and eventually the town became famous for one of England's greatest horse fairs. For one lively, lawless week in August a motley throng of fairground entertainers, card sharps, petty criminals and prostitutes mingled with hundreds of horse dealers. When they left, Horncastle resumed its role as a modest market town where corn and wool from the surrounding villages had been dispatched along the Horncastle Canal since the 1790s.

Between 1845 and 1847 there were six unsuccessful proposals to put Horncastle on the railway map including a Great Northern branch from Tattershall which Parliament rejected. As compensation the Company provided a wharf and warehouse at the canal basin. Something better was clearly required, so in 1853 local interests formed the Horncastle & Kirkstead Junction Railway and the GN readily agreed to work the line for half its income. Immediately the canal proprietors launched a vigorous but ill--fated campaign to persuade Horncastle's traders that a railway would harm them. Construction of the 7½ mile branch began in March 1855 and was a straightforward task, requiring only modest earthworks and a solitary overbridge spanning the summit cutting near Martin. On 11th August 1855 Horncastle celebrated the completion of its railway with a parade through the streets.

The town took to its branch line immediately.

Within days trains were bringing visitors to the horse fair and after a few weeks coal prices dropped markedly. The railway became very much a part of the community; a day at Lincoln or Boston market was suddenly feasible and by the early 1900s the town became virtually deserted during summer holidays as families headed for Skegness. For nearly 70 years a GN 0–4–4 tank engine was allocated to the tiny Horncastle shed for exclusive use on the five or six mixed passenger and goods trains which ran daily, except Sundays. The pace was sedate: a gentle climb from Kirkstead, followed by the run across the heath through birchwood and bracken, then the gradual descent into the broad Bain valley took 22/23 minutes. But service was much more important than speed, and the Horncastle Railway remained popular and profitable until it lost its independence to the LNER on 1st January 1923.

An intermediate station was provided at Woodhall. Although this was merely a hamlet at the time, a distinguished future was in store. Before the railway arrived, a local eccentric called John Parkinson dug a deep pit in an attempt to find coal. Instead, water rich in iodine and bromine was discovered and this gained a reputation for healing sick horses and curing gout. Then suddenly in the 1880s Woodhall developed into a fashionable spa town boasting a hydropathic establishment, hotels and scores of fine houses. It was said that upper class patients arrived hobbling, but soon took part in the village sports and nailed their crutches to the bathhouse wall before leaving! Woodhall Spa station was rebuilt with a passing loop in 1888 to cope with the influx of visitors and the line was improved generally. Spas fell out of favour in the 1920s and strenuous efforts were made to promote Woodhall as a golfing centre and holiday resort. Through carriages were provided from London King's Cross, and Kirkstead station was renamed Woodhall Junction on 10th July 1922.

Agriculture and its associated activities were responsible for the majority of goods traffic on the branch. Besides the horse fair there were sheep and cattle sales – in the early 1900s these generated up to 30 special livestock trains a day. The yard and goods shed received foodstuffs, farm machinery and coal, whilst the pens and loading dock dispatched animals and grain. Private sidings to a corn mill and malthouse saw

regular use. In the early 1950s there was still plenty of freight and the engine which had brought the afternoon passenger train into Horncastle usually went off to shunt the sidings ready for the evening goods. But all was not well on the passenger side. Local people had taken to the roads and despite strong objections the service was withdrawn on 13th September 1954. Trains ceased to back into the bay platform at Woodhall Junction for connections to Lincoln, Boston or Skegness and the elderly twin coach set, E44161/2, specially allocated to the branch retired gracefully. These saloons had originally been part of GN steam railcars built in 1905.

Horncastle continued to deal with goods traffic long after the passenger service finished. Coal was still delivered in some quantity, as it had been since the line opened, but agricultural requirements now included petrol, lubricating oils and tractor tyres reflecting the changed nature of farm machinery. Although deprived of its original purpose, the station building remained as dignified as ever. The big two storey block with its low pitched roof, tall chimneys and grand stone entrance dated from 1855. A single storey extension with even taller chimneys was added in 1900 and this survived as well. The only casualty had been a canopy roof over the platform which was removed in the 1930s.

Woodhall Spa's goods siding closed on 27th April 1964 and by the late 1960s road transport had made the branch virtually superfluous. Just one part time worker remained at Horncastle to deal with public deliveries, and the diesel shunter hauling its trip working from Lincoln Holmes Yard ambled cautiously over indifferent track, pausing frequently as the guard opened and closed seven sets of crossing gates. This time consuming operation lost money of course, and finally ceased on 6th April 1971. Once the Horncastle Railway was dismantled, Lincolnshire County Council purchased the trackbed and a section from Martin Moor to the outskirts of Horncastle was converted into the Spa trail footpath. Woodhall Spa with its moors of heather and gorse, its miles of woodland walks and its opulent Victorian houses remains a popular place to live, but almost every trace of the railway which created the town has been obliterated. For a while Horncastle station remained in use as offices, but, in January 1985 the demolition gang moved in here as well.

One of Woodhall Spa's greatest assets was its beautiful woodland setting and this was clearly visible from the 8.55 am from Horncastle to Woodhall Junction on 29th April 1954. A crossing house in the distinctive Horncastle Railway style is all that remains of the branch at Woodhall Spa. Photograph R.M. Casserley.

Having shunted the goods yard at Donington on Bain, class J11 0-6-0 No.64323 shrouded the station in smoke as it set off from Louth on 10th April 1951 (above). The track climbed up to the 557 yard High Street tunnel in the distance and Withcall tunnel (971 yards) behind the camera. Photograph Mick Black.

Louth C12 4-4-2 tank No.67379 was specially cleaned for the last day of passenger service (left) and the engine looked proud as it drew out of Wragby with a Louth to Bardney train on 3rd November 1951. Photograph A.G.W. Garraway.

Chapter 16
The Wolds

Immediately beyond Horncastle the land rises towards the Wolds. These chalk uplands, which are 13 miles wide between Wragby and Louth, reach 550 ft. near Caistor – a dizzy height for Lincolnshire! Ancient burial grounds and trackways lend an air of mystery to the remoter parts, but in medieval times the more sheltered valleys were well populated and fleece from Wolds sheep was the most valuable in England. This has long been regarded as the most beautiful area of the county, yet it is still comparatively unknown. Those who do explore it may be rewarded by a glimpse of Lincoln cathedral or Louth parish church in the distance, and when stubble burning was allowed an autumn sunset through the haze can be breathtaking.

Local interests were eager to fill the gap in Lincolnshire's railway system caused by the Wolds and obtained Parliamentary sanction for the Louth & Lincoln Railway during the 1866 session. A 10% dividend on ordinary shares was confidently predicted. The Great Northern agreed to work the line for 50% of its takings but were decidedly unhappy about its potential. Their fears were justified. Appalling weather, problems with Withcall tunnel and arguments with the contractor prolonged construction work, whilst difficulties with land purchase dic-

tated a south facing junction with the 'loop' at Bardney rather than a direct approach to Lincoln. In 1870 the company lost heart and tried to abandon its project, but permission was refused. Passenger services began at long last on 1st December 1876 – over ten years after they were authorised. Not surprisingly the Louth & Lincoln never earned enough to pay the interest on its bank loan, and in 1883 the GN grudgingly bought it at a knock down price. Ill–conceived and bankrupt it may have been, but the Louth to Bardney branch developed into a railway of immense character.

Stations and passenger trains alike became the focus of rural life for Wragby, Donington–on–Bain and other villages within reach of the line. Conversely, railway business was conducted in a way which reflected the leisurely pace of these farming communities. Four trains each way were sufficient, and this was reduced to three in World War Two Engines displaced from King's Cross suburban duties often worked across the Wolds, the last examples being Ivatt 4–4–2 tanks which were allocated to Louth shed from the 1920s. These class C12s became synonymous with the line until its closure to passengers. For many years they hauled old GN six–wheel carriages, long retired from the main line, although pensioned off rolling stock of Great Central, North Eastern and even North British origin appeared towards the end.

The promoters expected to see coal trains crossing the Wolds on the way to Grimsby docks and envisaged an ironworks at Donington-on-Bain using local ore. Thankfully the railway failed to stimulate heavy industry and it never became

a trunk route. Instead, from its opening to its eventual demise, the line served local farmers – giving them an advantage over those in Wolds villages further afield. Most stations had several sidings, a cattle pen and a loading dock whilst traders in everything from cattle cake to agricultural machinery established premises next to the railway. There was never any hurry – passenger trains took precedence on the lengthy single track and the pick–up goods often took over 3 hours to reach Lincoln from Louth.

As far as the railway was concerned, little changed between Bardney and Louth for 70 years, and even in summer 1951 there was little to indicate the imminent demise of passenger services. Imagine the scene on a sweltering afternoon as a train from Lincoln arrives at Bardney. Several passengers alight and walk across to the two–coach branch line connection. A leather strap is unhooked and a window dropped to allow air into the compartment. At 1.50 p.m. the simmering C12 comes to life and eases its train round the sharp curve away from the 'loop' line. Initially the track passes fields of ripening corn hemmed in by a wooded horizon, and a steady 40 m.p.h. is maintained. A few people leave or join the carriages at Wragby, the most important intermediate station. East Barkwith is less busy. So far the line has only climbed 130 ft. in nine miles, but the Wolds rise away in the distance. After its 2.08 p.m. departure, the C12 begins to feel the steepening gradient and beyond South Willingham the hills really begin to close in. Soon the train plunges into High Street tunnel and a sharp descent into the Bain valley provides a brief respite. The most beautiful part of the journey follows the 2.21 p.m. departure from Donington–on–Bain, although a 1 in 65 climb through the steep wooded confines of the Stenigot estate taxes the engine, even with just two coaches. Exhaust beats echo off the hillsides until the valley ends abruptly in a tree capped slope and the ascent towards the 400 ft. summit continues with a muffled roar inside Withcall tunnel for which the window is raised again. Steam is shut off as the train emerges in the isolated Withcall valley and the coaches sway and creak as they take the bends at 50 m.p.h. on the descent to Louth. Arrival is at 2.37 p.m. after the 21½ mile journey.

Closure to passengers was effective from 5th November 1951. Goods services were maintained for a while – usually at an even more leisurely pace than before – with the final section from Wragby to Bardney finishing on 1st February 1960. Since then much of the trackbed has been obliterated, though all the station buildings survive except Kingthorpe. Withcall, dating from 1882, is just a simple timber shed, but the others are far more substantial. Initially they appear rather plain. Closer scrutiny reveals otherwise, for there are some truly delightful details such as the bay window and clock hood at Wragby. Some stations were built of buff bricks, others of red bricks. However, each had courses of the alternative colour applied at different levels and in varying thicknesses – a wonderful frivolity for such an impoverished railway!

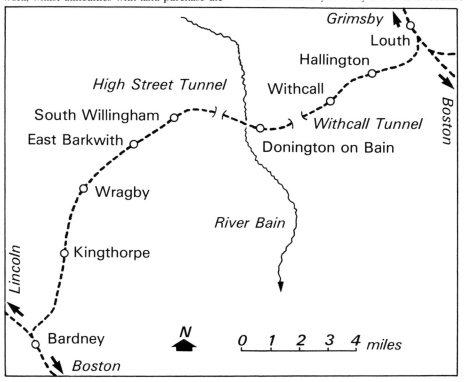

With a full head of steam but several leaking glands, class J11 0-6-0 No.64346 had its work cut out moving the Lincoln Holmes Yard to Firsby pick up goods out of Tumby Woodside on 19th July 1961. With the abolition of Coningsby crossover several years later, the short workings from Lincoln Central were extended to Tumby Woodside giving this remote Fenland village a very generous service of 26 trains a day. Photograph D.B. Swale.

On 11th July 1959 class B1 4-6-0 No.61388 rushed past the rain-soaked shrubberies at New Bolingbroke in charge of the 8.20 am Saturdays only Manchester Central to Skegness holiday train. The buildings had already lost their canopies, somewhat spoiling the appearance of the station. Nevertheless, thirty years later the platforms and most railway structures still survive here. Photograph H.B. Priestley.

Class K3 2-6-0 No.61938 drifted into Stickney with the 12.03 pm local service from Skegness to Sheffield Victoria, also on 11th July 1959. The oil lamps bearing the station name were a particularly delightful feature of this line. Stickney station is now a picnic area and the road overbridge has been removed, a house, cottage and goods yard buildings remain. Photograph H.B. Priestley.

Chapter 17
The New Line

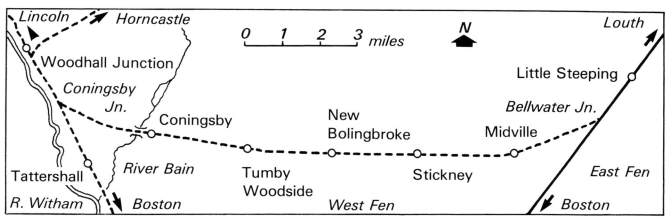

Coningsby Church

A few miles south east of Horncastle the Wolds end abruptly and overlook a huge expanse of Fen stretching away towards Boston. This was once a wilderness of rough grazing, morass and water where the River Witham struggled to reach the Wash. Life was hard for the Fenmen and even the sheep had to survive foot rot, lethal thistles and rustlers. Early drainage attempts were met by riots and a threat to burn down Boston, but in the 1800s reclamation proceeded steadily and peacefully. Eventually the present–day Fen landscape emerged – an immense plain criss–crossed with dykes and straight roads, and dotted with red brick farmhouses protected from the wind by clumps of trees. A feeling of emptiness prevails, and when the wide horizon has a backcloth of blue sky and ever–changing clouds there is an ethereal magic about this part of Lincolnshire. Such was the setting for the 'New Line'.

The Great Northern had no particular desire to serve the area, but it did wish to shorten the journey between Lincoln and Skegness – especially for holiday traffic from Yorkshire which had to reverse at Boston. Proposals to build an avoiding spur at Boston and a direct line across the Wolds from Horncastle to Spilsby had waxed and waned back in the 1880s, but by 1911 the GN had decided that something really had to be done. The outcome was 15 miles of double track forming a cut off between the 'Loop' and East Lincolnshire routes. The Kirkstead & Little Steeping line took 16 months to build and passenger trains commenced on 1st July 1913.

Five local stations were provided at remarkably regular intervals along the line, and each place served had a distinctive character. Coningsby is a small town famous for its big one–handed church clock whilst Tumby Woodside is a tiny village within sight of extensive plantations bordering the Fens. John Parkinson, besides hankering after a coal mine at Woodhall, decided to create an industrial city – and that materialised as New Bolingbroke! Stickney dates from medieval times and is strung along a low ridge separating West and East Fen, whilst Midville was a creation of the drainage schemes and its lonely station stood in deepest Fen country.

As usual there were celebrations when the line opened, particularly at Stickney where nearly everyone took a trip to Skegness. But the euphoria was short lived. The newly–built line had one of its tracks removed for use at the World War 1 battlefront, but the ship carrying them was sunk. Nevertheless, every station remained open and from 1923 onwards the reinstated and upgraded line began to justify the money spent building it. Seaside trains steamed across the Fens at a steady 40 m.p.h. and a stopping service of four or five trains each way catered for local residents.

Fenland soil is immensely fertile and the reclaimed levels have always yielded a rich bounty of produce. The GN had this hinterland in mind when goods facilities were installed at the five stations. Each consisted of a long siding for cart traffic together with a small loading dock for animals and agricultural machinery. Large industrial consignments were not anticipated, so a small weighbridge and office together with tranship shed in the platform buildings substituted for a full size goods depot. For a while traffic was plentiful, with Tumby Woodside gaining a widespread reputation for the despatch of potatoes.

Until the early 1960s, holiday trains from places such as Sheffield Victoria, Bradford Exchange and Manchester London Road continued to disturb the rural tranquillity of the New Line stations on their way to Skegness and Mablethorpe. But the total obliteration of east Lincolnshire's railways proposed for January 1964 inevitably included the Kirkstead & Little Steeping section. The ensuing uproar over hardship, particularly at Skegness, gave the route a stay of execution. Its western extremity actually enjoyed something of a revival when extra Lincoln – Coningsby services were provided for the nearby RAF base following the closure of Tattershall station on the Boston line. Goods facilities were withdrawn on 30th March 1964 and the stations became unstaffed halts on 7th October 1968. Diesel multiple units rolled forlornly across the Fens and increasingly gave the impression of living on borrowed time. The distant Wolds were the same as ever, but precious few passengers now boarded or alighted at the five stations. The battle to save the line was finally lost on 5th October 1970.

At the end, the New Line was remarkable in that it survived much as built – a working museum of late GN years. The stations still had their original interior fittings, platform seats, signs and nameboards, and somersault signals on lattice posts controlled the trains. Inevitably there was some evidence of neglect – New Bolingbroke's shrubs had run wild and Coningsby had been daubed by the local layabouts for example. All five stations had a plain but distinctive office building which could be mistaken for the village hall, supplemented by a small amenity block on each platform. Because of the road overbridge rather than level crossing at Stickney, the former was down a driveway not by the roadside. It was the most pleasing composition of all and even the harsh red brick and the green and cream paintwork looked quite fresh. After track lifting most of the formation reverted to farmland and few railways have disappeared yet left so much. As well as Tumby Woodside, New Bolingbroke and Midville station buildings there are over 40 distinctive dwellings. These are either detached houses with stuce gables or cottages with chamfered roofs in terraces of two, three or four and they are strung out in a kind of ley line across the Fens.

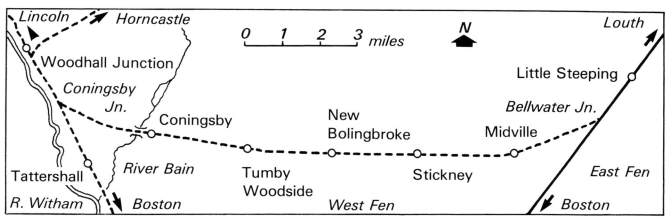

Besides the London expresses from Grimsby, there were several semi-fast workings to Peterborough over the East Lincolnshire line. On 11th July 1959 B1 4-6-0 No.61366 sped through Authorpe with the 3.24 pm from Grimsby Town to Peterborough North. The train had a couple of fish vans in tow and the engine displayed the silver painted smokebox door hinges characteristic of Immingham depot at the time. Photograph H.B. Priestley.

The original East Lincolnshire village stations consisted of neat two storey buildings which combined accommodation for the station master with office facilities. They featured low pitched roofs, fine chimneys, round headed windows in pairs and a small bay window overlooking the platform. Good examples can still be seen at Sibsey, Old Leake, Eastville and Little Steeping from the Skegness train. Willoughby, however, was rebuilt on the opposite side of the level crossing when the branch to Sutton on Sea opened. The sizeable timber building had a big umbrella canopy as can be clearly seen in this view from the station footbridge on 11th July 1959. Photograph H.B. Priestley.

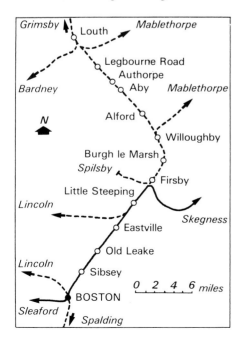

Alford Mill

Chapter 18
East Lincolnshire

North of Boston the Fens merge with the Marsh. Although this stretch of lush cattle pastures between the Wolds and the North Sea was reclaimed from desolate salt flats centuries ago, it was isolated and agriculturally backward when Parliament authorised the East Lincolnshire Railway's 47 mile line between Grimsby and Boston in 1846. The company expected rich rewards from opening up the Marsh generally and the old market towns of Louth, Alford and Burgh in particular, but also saw itself as an outlet for traffic from Grimsby to the south. George Hudson began to show an interest in the proposed line, so the Great Northern decided to lease the EL and guaranteed a 6% dividend to shareholders. In later years the GN's own shareholders voiced concern over this financial burden, but admitted that the prospect of the line in rival ownership was unthinkable.

On 1st March 1848 little 'Sharpie' 2–2–2 engines began to haul 4–wheel coaches between Louth and Grimsby. On 3rd September 1848 the line was extended southwards to Firsby and a month later trains began running to Boston. The

East Lincolnshire Railway was worked as part of the GN system, yet remained independent until absorbed by the LNER on 1st January 1923. Earthworks were relatively light and the only structures of note were a four arch brick viaduct over the Great Eau near Aby, together with a long bridge spanning the Steeping River south of Firsby. Level crossings were particularly abundant – there were over a hundred of them. But in terms of station architecture the line was exceptional, and Louth station in particular was a masterpiece. Alford and Firsby, although less imposing, were equally fine. Each consisted of a long single storey block flanked by two storey houses, but detail treatment varied and there was a marked contrast in the style of the projecting arcade. Both had an overall roof. Small stations were just as delightful, and even the many humble crossing houses were thoughtfully designed.

East Lincolnshire's market towns experienced a modest growth as a result of the increase in commerce brought by the railway. But passenger traffic generated by the growing coastal resorts proved far more important. The EL also became Grimsby's principal route to the south, as anticipated by its promoters, and King's Cross expresses travelled via Louth and Boston for 118 years. In addition the line rescued agriculture from its isolation, and from Louth to Burgh seven goods yards became railheads for farmers in the eastern Wolds as well as the Marsh. Further south, remote Fenland stations were equally vital outlets for produce, and in the sugar beet season

Eastville loaded up to sixty wagons a day. Through freight from Grimsby was heavy, and prior to the opening of the Great Central's London Extension most southbound fish traffic came this way. Iron ore trains from High Dyke to Scunthorpe also used the EL to avoid a reversal at Lincoln.

Beeching was particularly cruel to east Lincolnshire, for virtually every line was recommended for closure. At the time it seemed inconceivable that the King's Cross expresses would cease and that Grimsby and Boston would be left as the only stations for the whole of the Lincolnshire coast. Old Leake station had perished in 1956 and the stopping service was further amended on 11th September 1961 with the closure of numerous small stations. But the wholesale destruction proposed in 1963 was not allowed to take place without a fight. The arguments naturally focused on passenger facilities, and the abandonment of most local goods yards in 1964, followed by the last freight trains to Alford, Burgh–le–Marsh and Willoughby in April 1966, went largely unnoticed. In the mid–1960s, with government animosity and BR apathy, the East Lincolnshire line stood little chance, despite its champions. Closure was at least staved off, but in the end even the rays of hope brought by the 1968 Transport Act failed to save it. Grimsby – Peterborough services finally ceased from 5th October 1970, although the Boston – Firsby section was retained in conjunction with the Skegness branch.

Class C12 4-4-2 tank No.67379 and its immaculate set of elderly Great Northern coaches waited in the bay platform at Willoughby with a local service for Mablethorpe and Louth on 25th July 1952. The brilliant display of blooms helped Willoughby win the 'best kept station' award year after year. Photograph J. Cupit.

Four views of Eastville on 19th July 1961 illustrate the variety of traffic over the East Lincolnshire line. WD 2-8-0 No.90189 trundled south with departmental hoppers loaded with slag ballast from Scunthorpe. Photograph D.B. Swale.

A very work-soiled B1 No.61207 rushed through with a Cleethorpes to Peterborough North semi-fast. The attractive 1848 station building is out of sight to the left opposite the rather primitive shelter. Photograph D.B. Swale.

When the steelworks at Scunthorpe used domestic rather than imported iron ore, much of it travelled over the East Lincolnshire line. Class 02/1 2-8-0 No.63923 passed Eastville with a Belvoir – Frodingham train. Photograph D.B. Swale.

The pick up goods was living on borrowed time in 1961 and Eastville yard, along with so many others, closed in 1964. Ivatt class 4MT 2-6-0 No.43085 of Boston shed had a light load. Photograph D.B. Swale.

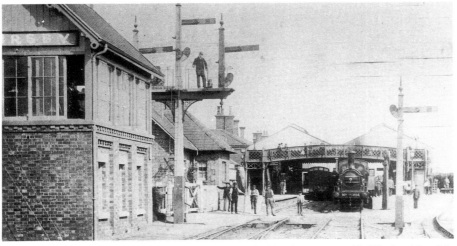

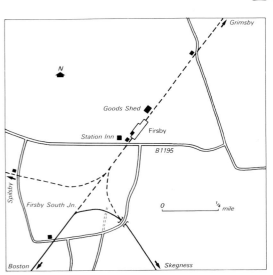

Firsby had one of the most remarkable stations in Lincolnshire. In common with Alford and Louth it boasted a grand facade and an overall roof, seemingly for a scattering of small villages but actually for the old towns of Spilsby and Wainfleet which were four miles away to the west and south east respectively. Eventually these acquired their own branch lines and Firsby became a junction of some significance. In this 1880s view Hawthorn 2-2-2 No.214 had just arrived with a southbound passenger train. Photograph courtesy V.R. Webster.

The Wainfleet branch was soon extended to Skegness and carried an increasing amount of seaside holiday traffic, most of which had to reverse at Firsby causing congestion and delay. So the curve from Firsby South Junction avoiding the station was opened on 24th May 1881. However, when ex-Great Central 04 2-8-0 No.6230 lumbered past the junction with a heavy northbound goods in October 1940 the coastal resorts were preoccupied with thoughts of an enemy invasion rather than an influx of holidaymakers. In 1941 this engine was one of 92 04s called up for service overseas. As War Department No.772 it left Britain in December 1941 for the Middle East. Two of its sister locos met a watery grave on the way, but 772 survived and entered service with Egyptian State Railways after the War. Photograph T.G. Hepburn.

by

Station Frontage

By autumn 1969 Firsby had been threatened with closure for over 6½ years but it was still served by London expresses – even on Sunday. One of these, the 10.52 Grimsby to King's Cross was eased under the overall roof by Brush Type 4 D1536 on 21st September 1969 as the connection for Skegness waited. At the time there were about fifty trains a day on weekdays with bursts of activity when several called within a few minutes, followed by long periods of inactivity. At least there was plenty of time for a pint of Bateman's 'Good Honest Ale' at the Station Inn which had wall prints of LMS(!) expresses.

Seen from the station footbridge on 23rd July 1952, class B1 4-6-0 No.61391 drifted into Firsby with a Peterborough North to Cleethorpes semi-fast as an A5 4-6-2 tank fussed about on the Skegness line. Since closure, every trace of the railway in this view has disappeared except for the original crossing house which was given the name 'East Lincs 31'. Most of the station itself has also been lost, including the projecting entrance arcade with its exquisite Italianate stonework and the overall roof support columns between the tracks, which had the best decorated ironwork on the East Lincolnshire line. The goods depot also survives and a sign stating 'Engines must not enter this shed' was preserved by the potato merchant occupying it – the railway still haunts Firsby! Photograph J. Cupit.

In this arranged photograph taken at Spilsby during 1890, GN 0-4-2 tank No.126 had just arrived with the branch passenger train. The parish church of St. James is prominent on the skyline and a few of the late 19th century houses and shops which were built near the railway can be seen on the left. Photograph Courtesy A.J. Ludlam.

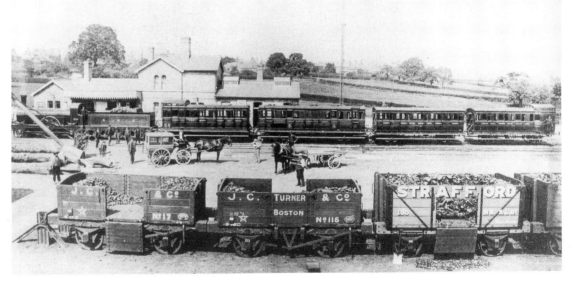

The atmosphere of the terminus and the nature of its traffic in Victorian times are captured well in this delightful view taken during 1886. Coal wagons were being unloaded in the foreground and Sturrock 2-2-2 No.210, dating from 1852, had worked the passenger service from Firsby. Railway staff and other workers posed alongside a delivery cart and the local horse bus. Photograph Courtesy A.J. Ludlam.

A portrait of the intermediate station at Halton Holgate in June 1950. The platform was looking slightly unkempt but there was still a modest amount of activity in the neat goods yard. Photograph Mick Black.

Chapter 20

Spilsby

Sir John Franklin

Sometimes goods traffic was very sparse, as was apparent from the length of the Spilsby pick up on 23rd July 1952. C12 No.67350 had just left Firsby. Photograph J. Cupit.

Spilsby was founded when a Danish farmer by the name of Spilli chose to settle on rising ground at the threshold of the Wolds, Marsh and Fens. Eventually the village became a focal point for the surrounding area and Monday has been a busy market day since Edward III granted the medieval Baron Willoughby d'Eresby a charter in 1302. Spilsby had a close association with the Willoughby family until Eresby Hall burnt down in 1769. As a consequence they moved to Grimsthorpe Castle near Bourne, though their memorials remained in the parish church. Occupying a rather more prominent position in the market square is the fine bronze statue of Captain Sir John Franklin. The Arctic explorer and navigator was born in the town and died in 1847 during an expedition which discovered the North West Passage between Canada and Greenland. At the time Spilsby was a thriving market town with plenty of handsome brick and stone buildings, but it was shortly to lose trade to places with easier access to the East Lincolnshire line. A meeting in 1864 sought to remedy matters and the Spilsby & Firsby Railway was authorised the following year.

The company never had a firm financial base. It had problems raising sufficient capital to build the line, and when construction work eventually started the initial euphoria had been replaced by the sobering prospect of having to operate at a profit. Nevertheless, Spilsby celebrated the opening of its railway with pealing church bells, plenty of bunting and a feast at the Town Hall on 1st May 1868. The Great Northern operated the line for 40% of its receipts. Eventually the GN had to provide financial assistance to the struggling concern, but the 1880s depression reduced agricultural traffic considerably and brought the S & F to the point of bankruptcy. So the company had no option other than to sell out to the GN with effect from 1st January 1891.

The Spilsby branch climbed from 28ft. above sea level at Firsby to 123 ft. at the terminus 4½ miles away, yet the first two miles were level, with only Lady Wath's Beck and the River Lymn as obstacles. Gently rising ground required a modest gradient through Halton Holgate, but for the last ¾ mile there was a snaking ascent at 1 in 66 which placed restrictions on the load that could be handled and sometimes taxed the motive power. A limited amount of passenger business was expected at Spilsby, so a single platform was deemed adequate. Goods facilities were more generous and included six sidings, a

goods shed and cattle pens. There was also a small engine shed.

During Victorian times the station was particularly busy on May Day when visitors arrived for the annual carnival with its procession and maypole dancing. There were still occasional excursion trains to Spilsby in the 1920s, such as the 1s 3d return trips from Skegness for the annual 'over the sticks' race meeting. Archie Osborne of Skegness remembers collecting his winnings on one occasion before the bookie realised there had been an objection and all bets on the horse were void. To Archie's embarrassment, the very same bookie got into his compartment on the return train and even sat directly opposite, but failed to recognise his travelling companion! Opportunities for such jolly jaunts lessened, and on 10th September 1939, just 7 days into World War 2, the branch was closed to passengers. It was only one of a range of economy measures throughout the country, but it meant that Spilsby was the first Lincolnshire market town to be deprived of its passenger trains. The C12 4-4-2 tanks which had worked the branch since the early 1920s then dealt with freight alone. Parcels, potatoes, corn and livestock were dispatched; sugar beet was sent to Bardney; and coal and oil were brought in although a lot of traffic had already passed to road transport.

Towards the end there were two brief flurries of activity. On 16th May 1954 Spilsby arranged a

very warm welcome for a Railway Correspondence and Travel Society special, and a bouquet of flowers was presented to Mrs. Forster, wife of the East Midlands Branch Secretary who had arranged the tour. On 19th November 1958 there was a regal finale as the Royal Train accommodating Prince Phillip was stabled overnight just round the curve from Firsby. Goods facilities were withdrawn eleven days later and the tracks were eventually lifted.

The branch was a classic example of a local line faithfully serving a small community. There was no large scale flow of passenger traffic, as at the seaside resorts, and the town never developed industrially. A certain amount of Victorian building took place, but basically the railway had little effect on Spilsby. Today, the market still flourishes and the pubs are lively, but few of the residents are aware that there were ever passenger trains and fewer still remember them. Even the station building was demolished over twenty years ago. Halton Holgate station still exists as a private house, although it has been substantially altered and modernised. Three crossing houses also survive, and as with most other locally-promoted Lincolnshire lines an attempt was made to relieve otherwise plain buildings with some modest decorative work. Arched doorways headed by a corbelled brick moulding were chosen in this instance.

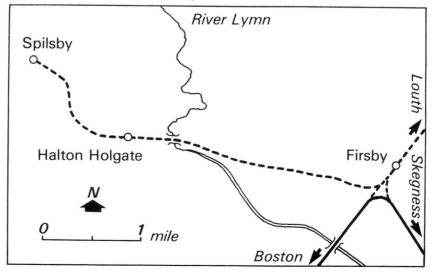

In evening sunshine on 12th September 1964 an ex-LMS 5MT 4-6-0 waited to leave Skegness with a return Blidworth Miners Welfare children's outing. The variety of trains in the station at the same time symbolised the transition from steam to diesel traction. On the right stood Brush Type 4 No.D1564 and beyond it was a B1 4-6-0 ready to head for the East Midlands. In the distance a 2-car diesel multiple unit was providing the local stopping service, whilst off to the left another Black 5 4-6-0, No.44918, was in charge of the RCTS 'Notts and Lincs' railtour.

As soon as the Wainfleet branch opened it began to carry a large amount of farm produce – in fact loadings exceeded expectations. Coal traffic also became important, especially at Skegness itself where sidings supplied local merchants for over a century. The Alexandra Road gasworks opened in 1878 also received a considerable quantity of coal. An incoming excursion headed by relatively new but decidedly grimy B1 4-6-0s Nos.61294 and 61229 passed the gasworks retort house on 19th August 1950.

Traffic levels had recovered from the trauma of World War I by August 1934 when ex-Great Central class B8 4-6-0 No.5280 prepared to head home from Skegness with a Bulwell Common excursion. The coaches were one of the LNER 'tourist' sets painted in pale green and cream. A more conventional varnished teak carriage is on the right. The fine GN signals on the left outlasted most of their contemporaries at the terminus and were still there when steam had gone. Photograph Ken Nunn.

Jolly Fisherman

One of the non-stop excursions from King's Cross made up of corridor coaches displaced from main line duties, headed by immaculate Ivatt Atlantic No.1427 is seen on arrival at Skegness in 1910. Photograph Courtesy Harry Wilkinson.

Warreners, fishermen and collectors of cockles and crabs were the sole residents of Skegness until a few affluent individuals began to venture there for sea bathing in the early 1800s. Some stayed at the local inn, which one disenchanted traveller described as 'vile and shabby and serving raw rank cold beef'. The transformation of this desolate coastline into a playground for millions began in a modest way. Wainfleet was a flourishing medieval port but Fenland drainage works finally put paid to its decaying harbour. Local interests were keen to see a revival and supported plans for a railway from Lincoln during 1845. The scheme foundered so salvation remained a dream. Spurred on by the success of the East Lincolnshire line, Wainfleet's traders tried again. This time everything went smoothly and the Wainfleet & Firsby Railway was authorised in 1869. Fireworks and marching bands celebrated the first passenger trains on 24th October 1871 and amid the euphoria there was talk of an extension to the village of Skegness, with holiday traffic in mind. The local company lacked the funds, and with an apparent monumental lack of foresight the Great Northern – which worked the Wainfleet line for 60% of its receipts – refused to help. Somehow, enough cash was scraped together and the railway to the seaside opened on 28th July 1873. Plans to revitalise Wainfleet harbour were quietly forgotten.

Skegness has often been described as 'bracing' – a clever way of capitalising on the chill wind which frequently blows in from the North Sea! But breezes have rarely been a deterrent to visitors and the line was an immediate success, vindicating the decision to build a three platform terminus. The 9th Earl of Scarborough, who was

the principal landowner, immediately began to develop Skegness as a residential resort. As the town grew its popularity increased: there were 75,000 visitors in 1878 and 110,000 in 1880. On August Bank Holiday 1882 alone, the GN brought in 20,000 people and turned others away when they ran out of carriages. Getting everybody home proved a mammoth task – departures were up to 7 hours late and someone from Leeds ended up in Nottingham at 3 a.m., but a good time was had by all. Such activity meant that the W & F was a healthy little concern when it passed to the GN on 1st January 1896. In 1900 250,000 holidaymakers arrived by train, Skegness station was rebuilt and the branch track doubled. Eight years later John Hassall's famous 'Jolly Fisherman' painting was used to promote non–stop 3s 0d excursions from King's Cross. During 1913 the branch coped with a staggering 750,000 visitors, but World War 1 burst the bubble.

By the 1930s traffic levels had recovered. In the town itself the 'jungle' was one of the many attractions and local young men made for the Casino ballroom during Players Week when Nottingham's factory girls flocked to the seaside. In 1936 Billy Butlin chose nearby Ingoldmells for

his first holiday camp. Then came World War 2, and another slump in visitors. In BR days traffic never quite reached the earlier peaks, but business was still brisk. Up to 40 holiday trains arrived from Leicester, Nottingham, Derby, Birmingham and London on summer Saturdays in 1955, so the 24 carriage sidings were still needed. Butlin's Redcoats met the trains and at the holiday camp itself custard-pie throwing, fancy dress frolics by the pool and bathing beauty contests were in full swing. With its genteel villas, tree lined Lumley Road and open carriage rides, Skegness has often attempted to portray itself as a dignified holiday venue. In reality it has always been a raucous working class resort, and most people love 'Skeggy' as such.

Proposed closure of the Skegness branch in 1964 came as a hammerblow to the town, as a third of all holidaymakers still arrived by rail. Up until then the only casualty had been remote Seacroft station, originally rejoicing in the name of Cow Bank, which had succumbed in 1953. It eventually became a pet crematorium, only to burn down in 1978 after the conclusion of the day's business! Goods services ceased in May 1966 and the local DMU's became paytrains on 7th October 1968. Opposition to closure was prolonged and dogged. As a result Skegness was the only Lincolnshire town to deflect the Beeching axe. When most of east Lincolnshire's passenger services disappeared on 5th October 1970, the link to the seaside via Firsby south curve was retained. Excursions continued and were hauled by a wide variety of diesel motive power, notably pairs of English Electric Type 1 freight locos, which became a familiar sight on holiday trains from the East Midlands right up until 1992.

In order to economise on signalmen's wages, Skegness trains were restricted to a single 10 hour shift from October 1977, leaving buses to provide early morning and late evening connections with Boston. However, BR and Lincolnshire County Council embarked on a jointly funded venture to provide automatic barriers at level crossings. The true GN flavour evoked by traditional signal boxes and somersault signals was doomed, but it seemed that the line itself was safe. Indeed the full timetable was restored during 1989 and in 1992 there were 16 trains each way on the branch. Meanwhile Skeggy stayed much the same, with what surely must be the greatest concentration of fish and chip shops in England!

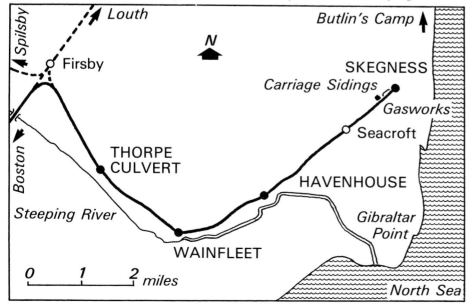

Not all Mablethorpe loop passenger trains were modest locals or holiday excursions. In early BR years a London express made its way round the loop, usually with a B1 4-6-0 in charge. On 1st September 1951 early morning sunshine cast long shadows and heralded a lovely day as No.61409 eased its lengthy train of Gresley corridor coaches into Mablethorpe forming the 8.07 am (Saturdays only 7th July to 8th September) Grimsby Docks – King's Cross. The train left at 9.09 am then called at Sutton on Sea before getting into its stride on the main line. Photograph J. Cupit.

The few engineering works on the loop consisted mainly of bridges over drainage channels. On 20th July 1955 class C12 4-4-2 tank No.67379 ambled across the girders spanning a dyke near Trusthorpe with a Louth to Willoughby train. The absence of passengers in the first coach even at the height of the holiday season is apparent. This bridge was one of those damaged by the 1953 floods and subsequently rebuilt. Photograph J. Cupit.

On 30th August 1951 ex-Great Northern class J2 0-6-0 No.65017 pulled away from Mumby Road with a Nottingham Victoria – Mablethorpe holiday express. Although the track layout might suggest otherwise, the train is taking the summer-only passing loop. Normally all services used the other line, as indicated by the signalling arrangements. The neat little Sutton & Willoughby Railway building is evident in this view, as is the station master's penchant for topiary!. Photograph J. Cupit.

Chapter 22

The Mablethorpe Loop

Mermaid and Dolphin

Much of Lincolnshire's coastline is marked by a ribbon of sand dunes, and it can be an inhospitable place at the height of an easterly gale. It was once the doom of many sailing ships, with locals gaining a reputation for plundering wrecks with gusto. There has also been a longstanding battle between the Marsh and the North Sea – the original village of Mablethorpe, for instance, was abandoned to the waves in medieval times. A vicious reminder of this struggle came with the disastrous floods of 1953, when present day Mablethorpe was completely inundated. Inland, normally safe behind the sand dunes, lies the rich Marsh pastureland and it was this that gave rise to the first railway to reach the 35 mile stretch of coast between Skegness and Cleethorpes.

In July 1872 the Louth & East Coast Railway was authorised to build a line from Louth to Mablethorpe. Little happened for over three years, and even when construction started it was a leisurely business. The branch finally opened on 16th October 1877 – worked yet again (for 50% of its gross receipts) by the GN. The original purpose of the railway was to serve farmers, but the potential revenue from seaside traffic quickly overshadowed this ambition. Therefore Mablethorpe gained four terminal platforms whilst the delightfully named villages of Grimoldby, Theddlethorpe All Saints and Saltfleetby St. Peter had to be content with one apiece.

In the early 1880s there were plans for a great fishing port to rival Grimsby. It was to be situated near the village of Sutton le Marsh two miles south of Mablethorpe, and in July 1884 the Sutton & Willoughby Railway & Dock Company was authorised. Despite a certain amount of haggling with the GN over working arrangements, progress was rapid and on 4th October 1886 the railway opened. Meanwhile, workers from industrial areas inland were clamouring for their share of North Sea breeze and many of them made for the newly rechristened resort of Sutton–on–Sea. An extension of the S & W to Mablethorpe was therefore logical, although the L & EC were concerned about the consequences. Nevertheless it allowed the newcomer into its station after modifications had been carried out, and the 23 mile loop between Louth and Willoughby was created on 14th July 1888. The fish docks never materialised, so Sutton's golden sands remained intact, and most holiday traffic used the line from Willoughby as the earlier company had feared. Both

the S & W and L & EC eventually passed into GN ownership – in 1902 and 1908 respectively.

The Mablethorpe loop helped local farmers considerably – for example it was far easier and cheaper to send cattle to Louth market. On the L & EC each small station had a cattle pen together with a siding and loading dock. Mablethorpe was envisaged as the railhead for a wide area, so facilities were more generous and included a brick goods shed together with a long siding for coal merchants. The S & W was extravagant. Cranes and substantial wooden goods sheds were provided at both Mumby Road and Sutton on Sea; at the latter the yard had no less than four sidings. Overshadowed by holiday traffic, the Louth – Willoughby pick–up plodded along day after day, year after year, delivering fertiliser and collecting livestock.

Over the years, loop passenger services were quite varied. Some of the 8–10 trains a day ran from Louth to Willoughby, but there were also Mablethorpe to Willoughby and Sutton to Louth workings. Certain summer trains were extended to Grimsby, Firsby, Grantham and even Nottingham. Elderly yet immaculate tender engines hauling rakes of six-wheel carriages were typical of the line in GN days, although a steam railmotor was used from 1905. From the 1920s to the mid–1950s C12s dominated the scene. The annual influx of holidaymakers brought more and longer trains, and there was also a greater variety of motive power, including rare visitors from far afield.

Even in the holiday season, the northern half of the loop led a tranquil existence. Brand new diesel multiple units replaced ageing C12s and other steam veterans on Mablethorpe locals in 1956, but as smart as they were, the DMUs had little chance of saving the route to Louth. When the driver had to slow for gates closed across the track and a friendly blast on the horn summoned a rather portly lady from her kitchen to let the train through, it was clear that little had really changed. Very few people used the intermediate stations and there was a feeling of despondency over their future. Facilities were duly withdrawn from the northern half on 5th December 1960. Closure of the southern part of the loop was proposed in 1963 and the pick–up goods ended on 30th March 1964.

Closure finally came on 5th October 1970 and subsequently much of the trackbed reverted to farmland. Nevertheless, several interesting buildings survive. The L & EC red brick stations were virtually identical to those on the Louth – Bardney line across the Wolds, even to the extent of having bands of buff bricks, although there were detail differences such as the treatment of decorative brickwork beneath the roofline. Besides the stations there were several delightful crossing houses. The now demolished S & W premises at Mumby Road and Sutton on Sea were fairly basic single storey wooden affairs, each with a full length canopy, fancy bargeboards and prominent chimneys. But the little company really excelled architecturally with its station houses. During the 1880s the 'Arts and Crafts' movement was producing some very distinctive buildings, yet it is amazing to find two fine, albeit small, examples in remotest Lincolnshire. They had huge, steeply pitched roofs finished with bargeboards forming a pointed arch, and the upper storey had tile hung walls.

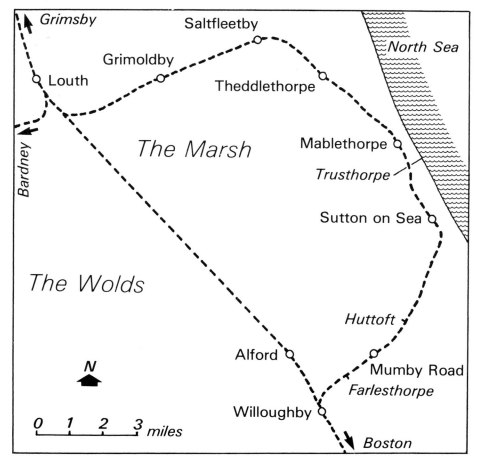

By the early 1960s Mable-thorpe holiday trains were up to main line standards. On 9th September 1961 B1 No.61209 simmered gently at the head of the 1.17 pm to Derby Friargate as its driver, his face etched with years of experience, enjoyed a cigarette and a chat to the station master. Photograph Horace Gamble.

In the 1950s the majority of summer extras consisted of non-corridor stock pulled by fairly vintage engines and prior to the arrival of diesel railcars local trains were mostly pure Great Northern. On 28th July 1952 C12 No.67384 rushed into Mablethorpe with a Firsby – Louth service as a brand new Ford Popular waited at the crossing gates and a few impatient pedestrians used the fine GN footbridge. Photograph J.P. Wilson.

Chapter 23

Mablethorpe

On the Beach

A break from the trains and back to the beach.

There is a vast panorama of sand, sea and sky from the dunes at Mablethorpe. It was here, sheltered by the marram grass, that Tennyson celebrated the publication of his first book of poems in 1827 by reading them aloud with his brother. They wanted solitude and could not have imagined how the village would be transformed once it had a railway. But holidays are happy times and GN publicity used the slogan 'Safe, Sunny, Salubrious – Merry Mablethorpe – the Children's Playground'. Eventually a continuous strip of built–up seaside stretched all the way to Sutton on Sea. Yet even today, when there are as many as 50,000 visitors on a fine sunny day, peace and quiet can be found in the more remote dunes.

Mablethorpe station was a very busy place on summer Saturdays in the 1950s. From mid–morning to early afternoon the trains arrived from Leicester Belgrave Road, Nottingham Victoria, Derby Friargate and elsewhere. If the ultimate destination was a flat or guest house in Wellington Road, parents burdened with heavy suitcases could just about cope with a short walk past the High Street shops where displays of buckets, spades, flags and windmills were a considerable source of excitement for youngsters planning the

best ever sandcastle. Meanwhile families bound for a caravan at Golden Sands boarded a Lincolnshire Road Car single decker and had no such distractions. Mother's first task was to un- pack the cases and father's thoughts turned to signing his family into the local club and having a quick pint at the Louth, Eagle or Book–in–Hand on the way. But every boy or girl who had pre- viously been to Mablethorpe was eager to find out if the sandhills, beach and helter skelter were still there on the other side of the 'pullover'. Ahead there was endless fun to be had from hectic sessions on the dodgems and feeding half- pennies into slot machines, whilst on the beach a donkey ride or trip on the sand train made a change from building sandcastles. A real adven- ture was the expedition north along the sands to where a derelict wartime gun emplacement and the red flag marking the start of a firing range provided a sinister contrast to Mablethorpe itself.

In the middle of a fortnight's stay, Saturday morning at the station was memorable for certain small boys. Returning holiday trains swallowed huge queues of people from the High Street and glum faces peering from carriage windows were a telling contrast to the cheerful expressions of children about to start their holiday. A fence next

to the level crossing was an ideal perch for observing these comings and goings, albeit with occasional reminders from father to sit still and therefore avoid falling in the stagnant ditch! At such close quarters, engines blasting over the crossing were rather frightening, yet utterly fasci- nating to those of tender years.

As the children of the 1950s grew up, Mable- thorpe's railways were winding down. In 1964 well over ¾ million people still visited the town by train, but otherwise an average of just 270 journeys a day were made on the branch – and most of these were during the summer. In winter the DMUs were virtually deserted. As local opposition to closure raged, there was ample evidence to suggest that excursion traffic was being deliberately discouraged. In 'Loxley House' Tennyson referred to railways as 'ringing grooves of change'. They had certainly changed Mablethorpe; depriving the town of its trains was, it seems, an underhand business.

On 3rd October 1970 coloured lights strung along Mablethorpe's High Street were a lingering reminder of summer fun as the nearby station prepared to deal with its very last passengers. It was a sad occasion, yet was offset by remarkable scenes as the final train prepared to depart. Crowds almost spilled over the platform edge, a mock funeral complete with coffin and pall–bear- ers took place, and the 19.55 for Willoughby was packed to bursting point. Throughout the next day the station stood silent and deserted, as was usual on a Sunday towards the end – but this time the trains never returned. Prior to closure, a couple of pensioners in a Mablethorpe cafe were bemoaning the loss of their railway, though they agreed that at least it would stop the rough ele- ment coming in. In reality, the lack of trains deterred very few people – the queues outside the station were replaced by traffic jams else- where. Nowadays the dunes north of Mable- thorpe are a nature reserve because of their rare plants and nesting birds, whilst sedate Sutton- –on-Sea has scores of bungalows occupied by retired people with memories of happy holidays by the seaside. Mablethorpe station has com- pletely vanished and its site is now occupied by a sports hall, market and houses.

For many years a class J11 0-6-0 was usually in charge of the loop pick up goods but on 3rd August 1951 C12 No.67381 was having a change from passenger duties as it made a spirited start from Mablethorpe on its way back to Louth. Photograph J. Cupit.

As has become apparent from earlier chapters, the C12 4-4-2 tanks were synonymous with East Lincolnshire branch lines prior to the introduction of diesel multiple units and one of the celebrities, No.67379, waits in the Mablethorpe loop bay at Louth. The cloud of smoke beyond the train is from an engine being prepared for duty at the loco shed. Photograph J. Cupit.

The Derby-built railcars intended for branch lines in Lincolnshire eventually worked services over the 78½ miles between Grimsby and Peterborough as well. On 8th January 1970 the 13.32 departure for Peterborough waited near the delightfully named Louth South signal box. The overall roof had long been removed but the main building was as handsome as ever. A blizzard which had raged over Lincolnshire earlier in the day gave the station a picturesque and seasonal look.

Another locally based C12 No.67383 waited at Louth with a mid-morning departure for Mablethorpe in August 1954. The overall roof and engine shed are clearly visible in the background. When they were removed this part of the station became somewhat open and bleak. Photograph John Clay.

Chapter 24
Louth

St.James's

Alfred Tennyson, future Poet Laureate and writer of the immortal Victorian ballad 'Come into the garden Maud', grew up in the Wolds village of Somersby and attended Louth Grammar School from 1816 to 1820. He found the latter experience distinctly painful, for the educational tone was set by the school seal depicting a boy being birched! Then, as now, Louth was dominated by its majestic parish church, the soaring 295 ft. spire of which can be seen for miles

around and pinpoints the old market town from both the Wolds and the Marsh. Shortly before Tennyson's time the local council had attempted to industrialise Louth by sponsoring the construction of a canal from Tetney. It opened in 1770 and for a short while an inland port rivalling neighbouring Grimsby was created. A boatyard and woollen factory began production and elegant Georgian buildings grew up around the wharf where coal barges were unloaded. In the 18th century Louth was too remote from potential markets to develop further, and the town had to wait for the East Lincolnshire Railway to provide the necessary communications to ensure its future prosperity.

The Great Grimsby & Sheffield Junction Railway made intense efforts to acquire the East Lincolnshire well before either of their lines were complete. As noted earlier the Great Northern offered very attractive terms, thus securing the lease. Potential traffic between Hull, Grimsby and London was the prime consideration, but eventually the line became the key to the coast and it is interesting to contemplate how Mablethorpe and Skegness might have developed had they been served by the GG&SJ's successors – the Manchester, Sheffield & Lincolnshire, and Great Central.

GN trains began to run from Louth to Grimsby and thence to New Holland on 1st March 1848. The first two months' operations generated £2,500 in revenue – a modest start towards recouping the massive £2½ million which the company had already spent on its own system. At Louth the EL built a magnificent mock Jacobean station incorporating its own headquarters, and the platforms were sheltered by a twin span roof carried on bracketed iron columns between the tracks. Within 2½ years the GN was operating out of London, giving Louth vastly improved access to the capital, and Hull's letters and parcels were travelling this way on the fast night mail from the Eastern Counties Railway's Shoreditch station.

Following the opening of the line across the Wolds from Bardney in 1876 and the Mablethorpe branch in 1877, Louth became a focal point for local passenger services. This was emphasised ten years later when a bay platform was added at the southern end in readiness for the completion of the Mablethorpe loop. The engine shed – which had existed from the outset and was somewhat unusually placed right next to the outer wall of the station – handled a good proportion of such workings over the years. In 1905 its quota of Stirling 0–4–2s and 0–4–4 tanks was joined by a new steam railmotor, but in the 1920s Ivatt 4–4–0s relieved of their principal main line duties, together with class C12 4–4–2 tanks displaced from London suburban work, took over most local traffic.

Local passenger services began to decline soon after nationalisation. The Bardney trains ceased in 1951; Louth shed closed in 1956 following the introduction of DMU's; the Mablethorpe branch finished in 1960; and the stopping service to Grimsby was withdrawn on 11th September 1961. King's Cross expresses and Peterborough semi–fasts continued. The former were hauled by Immingham B1s until steam had its last impressive fling in the form of Britannia Pacifics. When passenger services were finally withdrawn on 5th October 1970 distant Market Rasen was recommended as the railhead for Louth. However, the huge Associated British Maltsters works justified the retention of a branch from Grimsby. In its truncated form, the northern part of the East Lincolnshire line saw the occasional special passenger train such as the Branch Line Society's South Humberside Railtour of 11th March 1978. The six car DMU was allowed 1½ hours to travel from Grimsby to Louth; King's Cross expresses did the journey in 18 minutes twenty years earlier.

Traffic to the maltings ceased in December 1980 and subsequent track lifting ended Louth's 132 year involvement with railways, seemingly for ever. The magnificent station, often described as the most handsome edifice on the Great Northern, was left to rot. Its architectural merits have long been acclaimed. A very tall single storey central section was finished off with a steeply pitched roof and prominent two storey end blocks featuring curly Jacobean gables and ball finials. Pale cream freestone, notably for the balustrades and noble 'porte cochere', relieved the bright red brickwork. Perhaps understandably, such excellence was of little interest to certain local youngsters who saw the abandoned building as an ideal candidate for piecemeal demolition until it was restored in 1991 as part of the station area redevelopment. The Grimsby–Louth Preservation Society hopes to reinstate the track and run services between the two towns. Meanwhile Louth, with a population of 11,000, is the largest place in Lincolnshire without passenger trains.

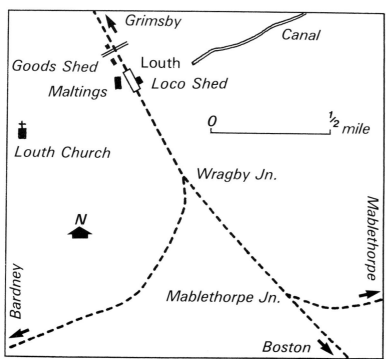

Something out of the ordinary always generated interest at Wellowgate. Elderly ex-GC J11 0-6-0s were a rare sight on heavy passenger duties in the mid-1950s, but at peak holiday times some depots were forced to use any engine that would steam. No.64372 forged over the level crossing with a return Cleethorpes special in August 1954 watched by a little crowd on the footbridge and an impatient B1 at platform 2. Photograph John Clay.

The weather was warm and trainspotting was a casual business at Wellowgate on 16th September 1961 when class 02 2-8-0 No.63923 trundled past with Scunthorpe – High Dyke iron ore empties. Trains occupying platform 3 often fouled the eastbound avoiding line, so it was little used by through freights. But this occasion was an exception – despite an apparently clear path on the main line. Photograph Roger Hockney.

Icelandic Cod

Despite a cruel winter and the gloom of post-war rationing there was a splash of colour at Grimsby on 24th June 1947. Apple green LNER B1 No.1195 set off for Cleethorpes with St. James church and the Yarborough Hotel as a backdrop. Photograph J.P. Wilson.

A thousand years ago a Danish fisherman called Grim decided to settle near a small haven off the Humber estuary. The resultant fishing village of Grimsby flourished in medieval times and the large parish church is a reminder of that prosperity. Less affluent times followed, but in 1796 the Grimsby Haven Company was set up to revitalise the silted up harbour. Once the new dock was completed Grimsby enjoyed a modest revival.

However, it was enterprise elsewhere that really determined the future of the town. By 1844 the Sheffield, Ashton–under–Lyne & Manchester Railway, linking the industrial areas of Lancashire and south Yorkshire, was nearing completion and demand for a line eastwards towards the coast was growing. Numerous schemes emerged but the successful one proved to be a continuation of the SA & M cross–Pennine line as far as Gainsborough, by the Sheffield & Lincolnshire Junction Railway and a further extension to Grimsby by the Great Grimsby & Sheffield Junction Railway. A line to New Holland, together with ferries to Hull, were proposed as well.

Local interest was strong from the outset, with Lord Yarborough of Brocklesby Hall becoming chairman of the GG & SJ. On 1st January 1847 the SA & M, S & LJ and GG & SJ amalgamated to form the Manchester, Sheffield & Lincolnshire Railway and the new company set about building its system east of Sheffield. The New Holland–Grimsby section opened on 1st March 1848 and sixteen months later MS & L trains could travel all the way from Manchester to Grimsby. Normally they did not, for New Holland was regarded as the eastern terminus.

Principal MS & L stations were impressive affairs with an overall roof and a substantial building facing the approach road. Architecturally they varied considerably. Some were remarkably ornate, but Grimsby had rather a plain brick frontage sparingly relieved by stonework. Initially the station proved to be something of a railway battleground. In an attempt to stifle any progress the Great Northern Railway hoped to make during its early years, certain rival companies persuaded the MS & L to join them in an anti–GN alliance known as the 'Euston Square Confederacy'. A general lack of co operation at Grimsby deteriorated into a situation where obstructions were placed on the track to stop GN trains reaching New Holland and in December 1851 such tactics succeeded. Relations eventually improved, but the service did not. There were just a couple of slow GN through trains to King's Cross and MS & L operations were decidedly branch line in character. However, from 1888 MS&L expresses headed for Grimsby rather than New Holland, and by 1900 the company had changed its name to Great Central and was running its own trains to London.

The early 1900s saw Grimsby's railways at their most colourful. Deep green Great Central locomotives hauling coaches in the new French grey and chocolate livery complemented bright green Great Northern engines with their varnished teak rolling stock. There were contrasts in motive power too. An Ivatt 4–2–2 usually headed the evening GN mail to Peterborough whilst the evening train to Manchester frequently had a GC 4–4–0 in charge. As World War 1 approached larger engines such as Ivatt and Robinson Atlantics began to appear. At the same time big GC 4–6–0s such as No. 424 *City of Lincoln* were rostered for the afternoon Cleethorpes – Leicester which was often a remarkable assemblage of three passenger coaches followed by up to three dozen fish vans bound for the Great Western. In the 1920s and 1930s Robinson's renowned Director 4–4–0s were a familiar sight as well.

The cramped layout at Grimsby, with busy level crossings either side of the station, has long been notorious. Frequent closure of the gates has always been inconvenient enough, but certain manoeuvres fouled busy Wellowgate for up to ten minutes and really tried the patience. Platform 2, the inner face of the island at Grimsby Town, handled Cleethorpes – King's Cross expresses, which reversed here. These trains loaded up to nine vehicles, thus forming a major cause of traffic delays at Wellowgate as the engine which had come in from the coast was uncoupled, and another – which had been waiting on the curve beyond Garden Street – backed on to the Cleethorpes end of the coaches. Problems of a different kind were caused by Platform 3, the outer edge of the island. It was used by some westbound services as well as local workings to and from Louth, but any more than three carriages obstructed the points at both ends.

Beyond the platforms were the avoiding lines, and during the 1950s and early 1960s there was usually excitement amongst the lads on Wellowgate footbridge when Garden Street box pulled the signals off for this route. Maybe an express fish train would come pounding through – a particularly impressive sight on the occasions when double headed Immingham K3s appeared. Alternatively, it might be a homeward bound Cleethorpes excursion with a rare B1 as a bonus. Smoke behind the houses away to the right was even more promising as it came from the East Lincolnshire line and often heralded an 02 or WD 2–8–0 straining to get a heavy iron ore train from High Dyke to Scunthorpe on the move.

In 1961 the London service received a boost when Britannia Pacifics Nos. 70035–41 were allocated to Immingham, displacing B1s from the duties. English Electric Type 3 diesels (later class 37) took over in 1964 but a few Doncaster–Cleethorpes turns remained steam hauled until late 1965. in 1970 the infamous reversal came to an end with the closure of the East Lincolnshire line and consequent diversion of King's Cross trains via Lincoln and Newark. Brush Type 4s (class 47) worked most of these until south Humberside entered the HST era during October 1982. Class 31 hauled trains from Manchester Piccadilly and Newark Northgate continued until 1984/85, but ever since there has been a virtual railcar monopoly. Meanwhile, twice a day, InterCity 125s continue to block Wellowgate for a couple of minutes.

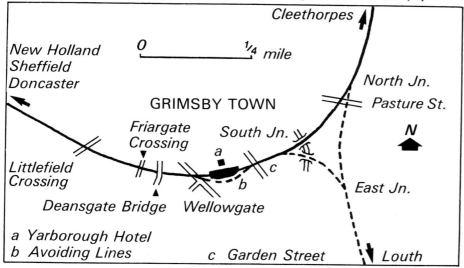

Cleethorpes

New Holland
Sheffield
Doncaster

0   ¼ mile

North Jn.

GRIMSBY TOWN

Pasture St.

Friargate
Crossing

South Jn.

N

a

Littlefield
Crossing

c

East Jn.

Deansgate Bridge   Wellowgate

b

a Yarborough Hotel
b Avoiding Lines   c Garden Street   Louth

On 29th December 1962 B1 No.61056 prepared to depart from Grimsby Docks with an unadvertised Immingham – Cleethorpes workmen's train. The unmistakable Spiller's building is in the distance whilst Grimsby Docks station itself was an undistinguished brick structure. A light covering of snow was beginning to melt in the weak sunshine, but the unsettled sky was an ominous warning of the big freeze of 1963 just a few days away. Photograph Roger Hockney.

Eventually the long running Banbury fish train became the 4.30 pm to Whitland and it is seen here on 8th April 1961 behind No.61905, one of Immingham's last K3 2-6-0s. Although not in the best of health on this occasion, the engine lasted until January 1963. In the background is the ornate Railway Hotel which was built in 1891 and demolished in 1978. Photograph Roger Hockney.

With the bitter winter just a memory, Grimsby Docks basked in warm sunshine on 4th September 1963 as B1 No.61158 eased a Doncaster – Cleethorpes stopping train round the curve at Cleethorpe Road Junction. For many years this was one of the busiest level crossings in the country, let alone Lincolnshire, and a policeman was usually on duty at the gates. The Dock Offices are straight ahead and the Royal Dock Hotel was off to the left. Photograph Roger Hockney.

Chapter 26
Grimsby Docks

The Hydraulic Tower

In 1845 the dubious assets of Grimsby Haven passed to a new Grimsby Docks Company closely associated with the Great Grimsby & Sheffield Junction Railway. The plan was to expand port facilities into reclaimed marshland beyond the Haven, but money was tight following the 'mania' and initially the MS & L could not fund it. However, when Prince Albert laid the foundation stone of the Royal Dock on 18th April 1849, a day of extravagant festivities more than made up for the delay. Commercial shipping began on 27th May 1852, followed by the branch line to Grimsby Docks and Grimsby Pier stations on 1st August 1853. The venture was an immediate success and

during the affluent 1850s more and more wagons carrying coal, timber and general merchandise were shunted along the quayside lines. In 1856 the first fish dock opened and a steady increase in catches resulted in the construction of Fish Dock No.2 in 1877. Eventually some 200,000 tons of fish was landed annually at Grimsby. Extensive sidings were laid out at New Clee to cope with this traffic and other tracks nearby received wagons laden with coal for trawler bunkers. Meanwhile the MS & L had been developing its continental shipping services and by the 1870s passenger steamers plied from Royal Dock to ports in Belgium, Holland, Germany, Scandinavia and even Russia. When Alexandra Dock opened in 1880 coal exports and passenger sailings were transferred from Royal Dock and the Pier station closed.

As the docks developed, a whole range of associated buildings and structures appeared giving the area its unique character. Most distinctive of all is the 309 ft. tower which provided water pressure for the hydraulically operated lock gates. Built in 1852, it was modelled on a medieval edifice at Palazzo Publico in the Italian city of Sienna. Today it is as much a symbol of Grimsby as the Stump is of Boston. Standing guard at the main dock entrance is the Dock Offices building of 1885. A slender tower forms its centrepiece, although this inevitably appears somewhat apologetic in comparison with the hydraulic tower. The ornate Royal Dock Hotel built in 1863 was just across the road, and a forest of cranes has always been a reminder of the business

at hand. Warehouses, transit sheds, ice factories, fish curers, marine engineers, chandlers and rope works completed the scene.

Despite the introduction of large diesel boats, there were still over 300 trawlers registered at Grimsby in the late 1950s. They spent up to three weeks at sea and in winter some braved the bitterest conditions imaginable off the Icelandic coast. About twenty returned home each night and what followed was a scene unique to the great fishing ports of the world. Barrows and clogs clattered over quaysides awash with slimy water and gut clippings to the accompaniment of loud chatter and squawking seagulls. Trawlermen's agents bawled the merits of their clients' catch as buyers' agents prodded piles of cod in huge trays. White coated auctioneers standing on upturned boxes spontaneously burst into high speed gabble, altering their tone in response to a nod, wink or twitch of the finger from those clustered around them. Meanwhile, trains of fish empties had been arriving at New Clee sidings and shunting engines fussed around the dock lines positioning wagons in readiness for loading. Just before midday, vans were attached to local Sheffield and Lincoln passenger trains at Grimsby Docks station while at New Clee an Immingham K3 was backing on to the heavily–laden 1.04 p.m. for Banbury. Then came a lull until the 4.48 p.m. to Nottingham, usually headed by an ex–LMS 4F 0–6–0. But over the next 3½ hours the fish really started to move, with three departures for King's Cross and others to Manchester, Leicester and Leeds. As the trains headed through the night another batch of trawlers rounded Spurn Head, their skippers watching for the welcoming lights of Grimsby.

During the early 1960s Britannia Pacifics and Standard 9F 2–10–0s brought super power to the fish trains, but all was not well. Over the previous thirty years road transport had captured most of the traffic and large firms such as Ross owned their own fleets. Rail strikes had not helped either. BR attempted to fight back with incentives and discounts, but the merchants were not impressed and fish traffic by rail finally ceased in 1967. Ironically, over the next couple of decades Grimsby's trawler fleet itself was virtually annihilated – partly as a result of the Icelandic 'Cod War'. There were also radical changes around Grimsby Docks station. The Royal Dock Hotel was demolished to make way for the flyover which replaced Cleethorpe Road crossing in 1968 and the station buildings were removed following de-staffing with the introduction of paytrains in 1969. Track was singled during 1985 and January 1988 saw the station footbridge cut up.

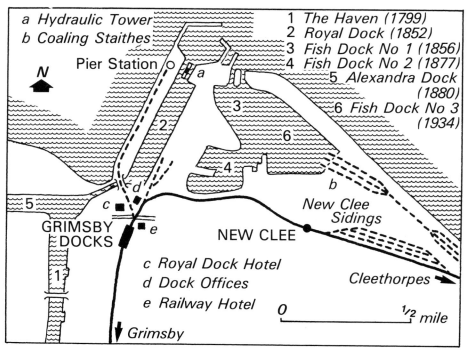

a Hydraulic Tower
b Coaling Staithes
Pier Station
N

1 The Haven (1799)
2 Royal Dock (1852)
3 Fish Dock No 1 (1856)
4 Fish Dock No 2 (1877)
5 Alexandra Dock (1880)
6 Fish Dock No 3 (1934)

New Clee Sidings
NEW CLEE
Cleethorpes

GRIMSBY DOCKS

c Royal Dock Hotel
d Dock Offices
e Railway Hotel

0   ½ mile

Grimsby

New Clee sidings were fully occupied with excursion traffic on 28th June 1959. The line up included five B1s, Nos.61208 and 61231 amongst them, and a couple of K3s – Nos.61803 and 61824. There were also two ex-Great Central class D11 4-4-0s Nos.62668 JUTLAND and 62660 BUTLER HENDERSON. These venerable veterans had worked excursions from Sutton in Ashfield and Kirkby in Ashfield respectively. Photograph Neville Stead.

During the early evening of 28th June 1959 JUTLAND was one of many engines to back its empty stock into Cleethorpes station. The backlog seemed to be causing a certain amount of inconvenience at Suggitts Lane crossing. On the left a few footplate crew were making their way back to other trains at New Clee, but a steady drizzle was setting in and the woman in the pakamac somehow says it all about so many days at the English seaside! Photograph Neville Stead.

On a fine Whit Sunday afternoon, 17th May 1959, B1 No.61316 made a lively start with a return Shirebrook West excursion. The Big Dipper in the background was one of a string of seafront entertainments which included the corrugated iron sheds of Wonderland – a children's paradise despite its appearance. There was also a ragged line of brick and concrete structures incorporating Hawkey's Premier Cafe boasting seating for 200 – mostly on the roof it seemed!

Chapter 27
Cleethorpes

Cleethorpes Pier

B1 No.61151 at Cleethorpes with the 3.59 pm to Sheffield Victoria on 30th August 1956. Hawkey's Premier Cafe overlooked the station on the left and the 1909 clock tower is in the distance. Photograph R.M. Casserley.

A century and a half ago there were just a few cottages and a couple of inns where the Humber mudflats gave way to the immense solitude of sand stretching away down the Lindsey coast. This little hamlet was called Cleethorpe, and in common with Skegness it was patronised by the fickle rich who seabathed despite a treacherous tide which came in for nearly a mile. The completion of the Manchester, Sheffield & Lincolnshire line heralded great changes. In 1858 for instance two 'monster' excursions arrived at Grimsby and thousands of working class day trippers were conveyed to the seaside by horse bus. The genteel retreated in dismay.

Cleethorpes, as the village became known, acquired a railway of its own on 6th April 1863 when a 2¼ mile single track branch opened from Grimsby Docks to a terminus almost on the beach. Double track was laid in 1874 as a result of the increase in holiday traffic, although even greater developments were in store. The MS & L had visions of a North Sea resort to rival Blackpool, so from 1880 the company spent over £100,000 on pier and promenade improvements, baths and boating lakes, and gardens and grottos. As elsewhere, an awesome regiment of seaside landladies emerged and the local council contributed everything from bathing machines to bowling greens. By 1900 the town had become one of England's great seaside resorts, a remarkable creation of the Railway Age. Nine years later the station was expanded considerably, and new buildings erected at the inner end of the platforms.

As Grimsby and Cleethorpes expanded they coalesced, and eventually the branch skirted terraced housing virtually throughout its length. An additional station opened at New Clee on 1st July 1875, and this remains open for trains bringing visiting football fans to Grimsby Town's Blundell Park ground which is actually in Cleethorpes. Local residents have always tended to favour transport facilities along the parallel main road – initially horse buses, then horse trams from 1881, electric trams from 1901, trolleybuses from 1937 and diesel buses since 1960. However, because of the restricted layout at Grimsby Town station, most Lincoln, Sheffield and Doncaster trains have traditionally commenced or terminated at Cleethorpes, so the service has been consitently generous.

In addition to helping Grimsby Town cope with regular traffic, Cleethorpes had to perform operating miracles when the annual influx of holidaymakers arrived. For over a century, summer Saturday timetabled extras, cheap excursions and factory charters headed for the north Lincolnshire seaside, mainly from the West Riding. They came from Doncaster, Sheffield, Rotherham, Barnsley, Wakefield, Bradford, Leeds, Pontefract, Mexborough and numerous smaller places such as Ryehill and Royston. Others started from towns in the Nottinghamshire/Derbyshire coalfield – Shirebrook, Clowne and Edwinstowe for example. In the twilight of steam B1s were usually in charge, but Black 5s performed regularly and sometimes a real stranger appeared. On 27th July 1958 no less than three ex–LMS Jubilee 4–6–0s arrived – Nos. 45597 *Barbados*, 45692 *Cyclops* and 45699 *Galatea*. An ex–LNER V2 2–6–2 was employed on Easter Monday 1961 and Stanier 4MT No. 42963 came in on 18th June 1961.

Saturdays saw the majority of timetabled extras carrying people to or from their annual holiday, but excursions dominated the traffic on Sundays and Bank Holidays. In the late 1950s there were still around 40 specials in a single day, and as many as 54 arrived on one memorable occasion. Once an excursion had arrived and disgorged its passengers, the train was backed into one of the stabling tracks between the station and Suggitts Lane. The engine then ran back to platform 6, took the road behind Cleethorpes signal box and was turned and watered before returning to its coaches. Many workings the proceeded to New Clee Sidings. During the evening one train after another backed down to Cleethorpes station, collected its happy throng, and set off smartly.

There was a rapid decline in holiday traffic during the 1960s and by the mid–1980s seasonal and special trains had been phased out altogether, for the local services from Sheffield, Doncaster and Lincoln were quite capable of carrying those holidaymakers still travelling to Cleethorpes by rail. In any case there has been a marked decline in the overall number of visitors during the last three decades. In 1985 the line was reduced to single track from Grimsby to Cleethorpes and the original plan was to retain just two platforms at the terminus. Fortunately the Operating Division over ruled the Civil Engineers and insisted on twice that number – wisely as it turned out, for sometimes all of them are in use. The original station building remains a prominent feature, but the proud Edwardian clock tower of 1909 is now overshadowed by the unsympathetic bulk of an amusement hall. Cleethorpes and its railway have certainly changed, but at least Steele's Corner House in the Market Place still serves generous helpings of fish and chips.

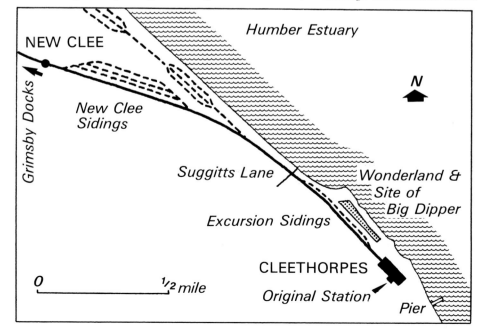

NEW CLEE

Humber Estuary

Grimsby Docks

New Clee Sidings

N

Suggitts Lane

Wonderland & Site of Big Dipper

Excursion Sidings

CLEETHORPES

0   ½ mile

Original Station

Pier

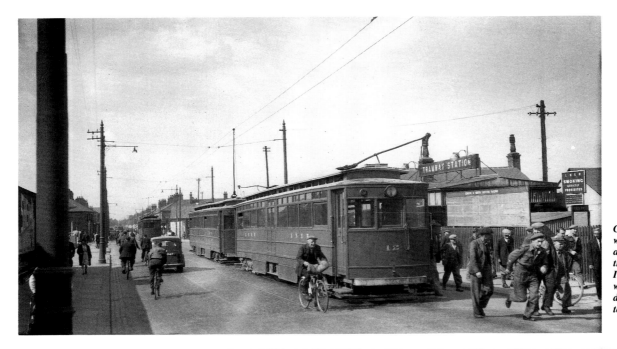

Corporation Bridge in Grimsby was a busy place at shift change, as on 6th September 1947. By then the cars of the Grimsby & Immingham Electric Railway were visibly ageing and wore a drab LNER brown livery. Photograph V.R. Webster.

A5 4-6-2 tank No.69820 waited at Immingham Dock with a mixed collection of rolling stock forming the 2.45 pm to New Holland Pier on 3rd June 1952. When services were finally withdrawn in 1969 the platform was usually hidden behind rows of bogie oil tank wagons, but somewhat remarkably the building was still there twenty years later, albeit in poor condition. Some good Great Central Edwardian styling can be seen in the station house at nearby Killingholme which is quite a contrast to the 1848 Tudor on the New Holland and Grimsby lines. Photograph John Edgington.

British Railways spruced up the Immingham trams with a coat of bright green paint and no doubt No.15 added a splash of colour to this dismal Grimsby scene in the early 1950s. The Spillers building and Albatross Mill loomed through the mist and the Palace Theatre across Corporation Bridge was still a popular venue. Corporation Road has changed a lot but the building on the left survives and there are still metal poles in Gilbey Road towards Cleveland Bridge. At Immingham several concrete masts and a couple of waiting shelters can be found. Photograph National Railway Museum.

Chapter 28
Immingham

Pilgrim Fathers

When the Pilgrim Fathers set sail from the tiny village of Immingham during 1608 in their second attempt to escape persecution, the area north west of Grimsby was a broad stretch of remote marshland bordering the Humber. Three centuries later enterprise of a different kind was about to transform this piece of riverside completely. At Grimsby, Alexandra Dock had opened in July 1880 and helped to relieve the congested Royal Dock, but coal exports, timber imports and general traffic continued to grow relentlessly. Furthermore, by 1900 sixteen railway owned passenger steamers regularly used the port. Further expansion was essential, and because much larger vessels were coming into use the Great Central ultimately selected Immingham where the deep water channel swung close to the shore and land was very cheap.

Work on the £2½ million scheme began with great ceremony on 12th July 1906 and an immediate outcome was that Humberville or 'Tin Town' where the navvies lived became a tourist attraction! Formal opening took place on 22nd July 1912. it was a magnificent occasion, with King George V and Queen Mary touring the docks aboard the brand new GC paddle steamer

Killingholme which was painted in white and gold. Brilliant sunshine showed off multi coloured bunting and flags as well as the dress uniforms of the Territorial Army. Afterwards Immingham settled down to the routine business of commercial shipping, but that was soon changed by World War One and *Killingholme* was almost lost on active service.

Many miles of new track were laid in connection with Immingham Dock; first came the Grimsby District Light Railway in time to carry special trains for the sod–cutting ceremony. From a triangular junction with the Alexandra Dock branch it headed west across featureless and deserted countryside to the construction site. At first the GDLR was basically a contractor's line, although from 3rd January 1910 a GC steam railcar provided a passenger service between Immingham Halt and remote Pyewipe Road Halt 1¼ miles from central Grimsby. The Humber Commercial Railway from Immingham to Ulceby required a 1½ mile cutting near South Killingholme and was to be the main route to and from the docks. Goods traffic began on 29th June 1910, followed by passenger services on 15th May 1912. The Barton & Immingham Light Railway followed the Humber to North Killingholme then veered across to Goxhill, opening on 1st December 1910 and 1st May 1911 respectively. Passenger trains from Ulceby and Goxhill terminated at the bleak Immingham Dock station near Western Jetty. In the immediate dock area, running lines, sidings, yards and a large locomotive depot (completed in 1913) accounted for an astonishing 170 miles of track.

Of all the Immingham passenger lines, the most heavily used and best–loved was undoubtedly the Grimsby & Immingham Electric Railway. There had to be an efficient means of carrying the many dock workers living in Grimsby, so the GC constructed an electric tram-

way. It ran from Eastern Jetty (on the opposite side of the entrance lock gates to Immingham Dock station) and continued to Immingham Town – actually 1¼ miles from the village. After a reversal the line paralleled the Grimsby District for 4 miles before using Cleveland Bridge to cross the Alexandra Dock branch. The final mile along Gilbey Road and Corporation Road to Corporation Bridge terminus assumed the guise of a conventional street tramway. Grimsby – Immingham Town services began on 15th May 1912 replacing the GDLR steam railcar. The extension to Immingham Dock followed on 17th November 1913. It was a railway of great character. A frequent service was maintained for 24 hours a day by twelve 64 seat single deck cars, originally resplendent in fully lined-out varnished teak. On the long rural section they swayed along at a steady 25 m.p.h., sometimes passing a steam hauled freight on the GDLR, and occasionally pausing at one of the four request stops. At either end of the line there was a complete contrast – especially during shift changes when workers bustled around the trams, which ran in convoys of up to six.

Grimsby declined as a port under LNER ownership. The Liverpool – Grimsby boat trains ceased in 1923 and twelve years later all continental services were transferred to Associated Humber Lines of Hull. An even bigger blow came with the Depression which caused trade generally, and coal exports in particular, to slump alarmingly. The area needed a more diverse industrial base and in 1948 British Titan was the first of many firms persuaded to build factories on the Humber shore. Consequently there was a substantial increase in the number of people using the Grimsby & Immingham Electric Railway, and to cope with the demand three trams were purchased from Newcastle in 1948, followed by no less than 18 ex–Gateshead vehicles in 1951. As many as 19 cars were in service during peak period. Despite its popularity the tramway was doomed thanks to the connivance of BR and Grimsby Corporation. The street section was blamed for traffic congestion, so the line was cut back to Cleveland Bridge on 1st July 1956 and this considerably reduced its usefulness. Complete closure came on 31st July 1961, forcing workers to use the replacement Corporation buses which took twice as long. DMU's continued to run between Immingham Dock and New Holland, but this service succumbed on 17th June 1963. Immingham was finally deleted from the railway passenger map when the last trains to Ulceby ran on 4th October 1969. Grimsby docks are still busy, and imports include new cars, frozen food and Danish butter and bacon, but only a tiny proportion is carried by rail. Immingham presents a very different picture. The impressive port, with its four deep water jetties capable of taking ships of 34 ft. draught at any state of the tide, deals with bulk commodities. A frequent service of block trains takes iron ore and coal to Scunthorpe, whilst Railfreight also moves a huge tonnage of petroleum products including most of the output from the nearby refineries.

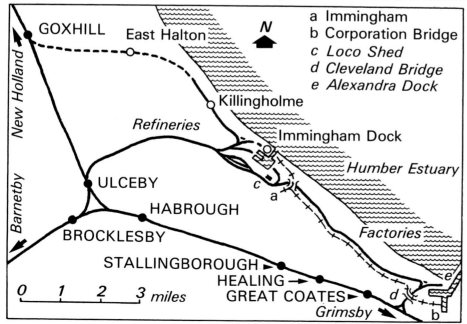

a Immingham
b Corporation Bridge
c Loco Shed
d Cleveland Bridge
e Alexandra Dock

N

GOXHILL   East Halton

New Holland

Killingholme

Refineries

Barnetby

ULCEBY

HABROUGH

BROCKLESBY

STALLINGBOROUGH

HEALING

GREAT COATES

Grimsby

Immingham Dock

Humber Estuary

Factories

0 1 2 3 *miles*

On 27th April 1954 B1 No.61142 waited at New Holland Pier station with the 9.58 am to Grimsby Town. The buildings are still there today under the shadow of giant ship-loading conveyors. Photograph R.M. Casserley.

Metro-Cammell 2-car diesel multiple unit E79051 and E79267 formed the 6.15 pm service from Barton on Humber to New Holland Pier on 22nd July 1956. The buildings at Barton station have long gone, but there is still a regular Humberlink train service meeting the buses to Hull via the Humber Bridge. Photograph John Edgington.

Chapter 29
Crossing the Humber

Humber Bridge

In Roman times there was a ferry known as *Transitus Maximus* where Ermine Street encountered the Humber, and around 1086 a Barton – Hull ferry was established. Despite the formidable water barrier Hull became an irresistible attraction for north Lincolnshire, and over the centuries sailing boats continued to brave the treacherous currents – though not always to everyone's appreciation. In 1725 Daniel Defoe described Barton on Humber as 'a straggling mean town noted for nothing but an ill–favoured dangerous passage, or ferry, over the Humber to Hull.....we were four hours tossing about'. A steam driven paddle sloop called *Caledonia* appeared on the Humber in 1814 and steam packets were soon operating from Barton. Fierce rivalry developed, notably between the *Royal Charter* which officially met the London – Hull mail coaches and the *Public Opinion* which also did, unofficially. External competition came from rival crossings based on South Ferriby, Barrow Haven and Goxhill Haven.

There was also a ferry from New Holland, a remote creek 3½ miles east of Barton on Humber which gained a dubious reputation for the import of contraband Dutch gin – hence its name. Road access was poor and it posed no threat to the other services until development work started in 1826. Ten years later the London – Hull mails were transferred to the New Holland crossing and by 1846 the ferry was carrying 70,000 passengers annually. In the same year the Great Grimsby & Sheffield Junction Railway

gained authority to operate paddle steamers from a 1500 ft. wooden pier to be built on the smugglers' old haunts. Passenger trains from Grimsby commenced on 1st March 1848, ten boats a day completed the link with Hull, and shortly afterwards New Holland enjoyed a glorious few months as part of the East Coast route to Scotland. At first, MS & L expresses terminated at New Holland, but when they were diverted to Grimsby in 1888 the line to the pier became a branch serving local needs, and as such it continued with very little change for nearly a century.

Barton's ferry struggled on valiantly after the railway boats commenced, but a branch line from New Holland to Barton on Humber which opened on 1st March 1849 did not help, and the ancient crossing ended in 1851. The railway had little effect on the old market town and Defoe's disenchantment would not be echoed by most people today. In fact its fine Saxon church and handsome Georgian houses make it one of the most attractive places in South Humberside enhanced by freedom of movement to and fro which its proximity to the Humber Bridge provides.

The Humber estuary is notorious for its shifting mudbanks, so paddle steamers with a shallow draught have always been essential for the New Holland crossing. Nevertheless the ferries had to take an indirect route to find a channel at low tide and sometimes there were long delays because of insufficient water even to float the boat at New Holland. Local opinion avers that on occasion the paddles actually acted as wheels. The MS & L began its operations with four second hand vessels – *Falcon*, *Magna Carta*, *Queen* and *Prince of Wales*. A distinguished succession of Humber paddle steamers followed, including the celebrated *Killingholme* of 1912. The final examples were ordered by the LNER – *Wingfield Castle* and *Tattershall Castle* were delivered in 1934 and *Lincoln Castle* arrived in 1940. Towards the end they were delightful survivors from a bygone era. Even on hot days a cool breeze developed as New Holland slipped away and Hull's waterfront grew closer, but when there was a bitter east wind only the very hardy would venture on deck. The snug little tearoom with its varnished woodwork and framed pictures was much more appealing than a lashing of icy spray whipped up by the churning paddle wheels. However, the last trip in the evening and consequent first morning trip from Hull had no buffet facility because the tearoom was staffed from Grimsby. That continued through MS&L, GC, LNER and also BR years. Watching the great piston rods at work was a fascinating pastime and occasionally it was possible to catch a glimpse of the Cornish boilers being stoked.

As early as 1865 a Humber bridge was mooted by Hull merchants frustrated by the North Eastern Railway monopoly, and they were back in 1872 with the Hull South & West Junction Railway which would have tunnelled under the estuary. This failed in Parliament, as did the Hull & Lincoln Railway of 1883 which featured a multi–span viaduct near Barton. Proposals for a Nottingham – Hull line between 1908 and 1914 were also unsuccessful. Separate road and rail tunnels to be funded by the Ministry of Transport and LNER respectively were suggested in 1932, but the latter decided to improve its ferry service

instead. The first proposal for a road suspension bridge came in 1935 and pressure continued until the government agreed to provide a 75% loan in 1971. Work began in 1973 at an estimated cost of £26 million and the bridge finally opened on 24th June 1981, four years late. With its ⅞ mile main span the structure is undoubtedly a spectacular sight, but by 1990 its cost was well over £50 million and rising monthly as tolls did not cover interest charges. The ferry, together with the train service along the New Holland pier, ceased on the same day that the bridge opened. New Holland Town station, once a fine red brick building with an ornamental stone entrance and an overall roof, became a melancholy scene of dereliction and desolation. Then in 1983 the area was transformed by New Holland Bulk Services. Town station was demolished, followed by installation of silos, conveyors and ship–loading gantries to facilitate grain exports via the old railway pier.

There is nowhere quite like New Holland. The long street of grey terraced houses dominated at the north end by the old Yarborough Arms Hotel owes its existence to the railway ferries. Today it is busy with road traffic to Howarth's timber yard and an endless procession of grain lorries, bound for the piers, whilst in the bar of the former hotel – now nostalgically renamed the Lincoln Castle – foreign accents of visiting ship's crews are commonplace. Happily the *Castles* themselves all survive. *Tattershall Castle*, withdrawn in 1972, can be seen on the Thames in London and *Wingfield Castle*, which last operated in 1974, is at West Hartlepool where it was built. *Lincoln Castle* suffered boiler failure in 1978 leaving *Farringford* (a diesel boat built in 1947 for the Southern Railway's Lymington – Yarmouth service) to soldier on as the bridge took shape in the distance. *Lincoln Castle* proved to be Britain's last paddle steamer in regular commercial use, subsequently found a home Grimsby's Alexandra Dock where it is now moored next to the National Fishing Heritage Centre.

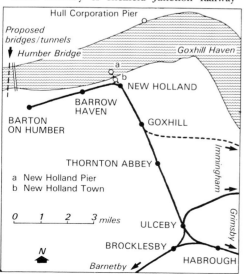

A Brush Type 2 diesel with iron ore empties taking the Immingham route at Ulceby on 21st April 1966. Photograph H.B. Priestley.

Map labels:
Hull Corporation Pier
Proposed bridges/tunnels
Humber Bridge
Goxhill Haven
a
b
NEW HOLLAND
BARROW HAVEN
BARTON ON HUMBER
GOXHILL
THORNTON ABBEY
Immingham
a New Holland Pier
b New Holland Town
0 1 2 3 miles
ULCEBY
Grimsby
N
BROCKLESBY
HABROUGH
Barnetby

In June 1963 track renewal was evident as a WD 2-8-0 eased its train of empty hoppers over the summit of Barnetby Gap towards the exchange sidings with Melton Ross limeworks. Woodland in the distance marks the edge of Brocklesby Park and the classical arch is just inside it. Although no longer rail served, the limeworks looks much the same from the A18 overbridge and continues to coat its surroundings with white dust. Photograph John Foreman.

Having cleared the summit of Barnetby Gap, B1 No.61112 romped through the cutting between Melton Ross and Barnetby East with a return excursion from Cleethorpes to Lincoln Central on a Sunday evening in May 1956. On such days there were between 25 and 30 specials through Barnetby, loading from 7 to 12 coaches. Photograph John Foreman.

Brocklesby Arch

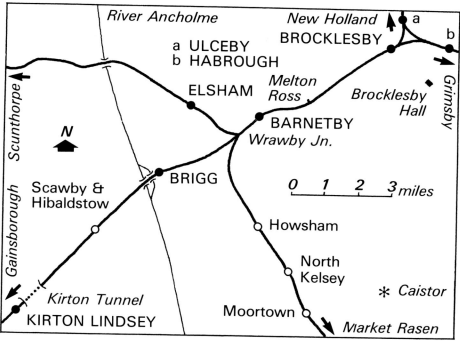

In the 1840s Brocklesby Hall had the third largest country estate in England, comprising some 50,000 acres. It was the home of the Brocklesby Hunt and a favourite venue for socialising aristocrats. Consequently, the 2nd Earl of Yarborough was a powerful and influential man, but he was also a model landlord whose programme of agricultural improvements had made his tenant farmers remarkably prosperous. Unlike some of his contemporaries, Lord Yarborough saw that improved communications would bring further benefits – hence his involvement with the Great Grimsby & Sheffield Junction Railway from the outset.

Between Grimsby and Gainsborough there are five distinctive bands of countryside running roughly north to south. The coastal plain gives way to the undulating chalk wolds which in turn overlook a clay vale drained by the River Ancholme. Higher ground returns in the form of an extension of Lincoln Heath and finally the River Trent flows in a broad valley forming the natural boundary of Lindsey. This was the country traversed by the GG & SJ's main line and Lincoln branch. Under Manchester, Sheffield & Lincolnshire Railway ownership, construction of the GG & SJ proceeded steadily from east to west. Completion of the Grimsby – New Holland line on 1st March 1848 was followed by Ulceby – Brigg and Barnetby – Market Rasen on 1st Nov-

ember 1848. The extension from Market Rasen to Lincoln, intended as part of the main London – Hull route but destined to become a minor branch, opened on 18th December 1848. Brigg – Gainsborough came next on 2nd April 1849. The Gainsborough – Sheffield section, together with the Brocklesby – Habrough spur were brought into operation on 16th July 1849 and one of Britain's greatest cross country trunk routes was complete. A line from Doncaster and Scunthorpe joined the others at Barnetby in 1866.

After crossing the Trent, eastbound main line trains climbed through Blyton and Northorpe towards the magnificent castellated portal of the 1334 yard Kirton tunnel. Although Kirton in

Lindsey itself was once an important market centre, its status had declined to that of a large village. The line then descended to Brigg which had enjoyed an increase in trade during the 1820s following improvements to the River Ancholme. In the distance the Wolds rose abruptly to over 300 ft. and railway construction could well have been costly. Fortunately the ridge dipped to below 100 ft. near Barnetby le Wold and provided an easy route to New Holland and Grimsby. Earthworks through Barnetby Gap were minimal and even the 1912-15 quadrupling associated with the development of Immingham Docks presented few difficulties.

Before the railway arrived, Barnetby was just

In low evening sunshine, B1 No.61313 of Darnall shed passed Scawby & Hibaldstow station on the original MS&L main line with the 7.15pm Cleethorpes – Sheffield parcels, during June 1956. The signal box, simply named Scawby, was demolished a couple of years later, one of the first in the area to close. Despite its relative remoteness from the villages concerned, the station remained open for passengers until 5th February 1968, although the goods yard closed in May 1964. Photograph John Foreman.

one of many small villages strung along the steep edge of the Wolds. In common with nearby Bonby, Bigby and Owmby, it had grown little since it was founded by Danish invaders nine centuries previously. Caistor, 6½ miles away, had long been the centre of local commerce but in Victorian times it had stagnated and Barnetby acquired several streets of incongruous terraced houses as railway workers settled in this remote fold of the hills. With the growth of Scunthorpe and Grimsby, Barnetby became an important junction.

The former GG & SJ lines displayed a fascinating range of architecture. Smaller stations were delightful red brick Tudor cottages with stone dressings: Blyton, Northorpe, Stallingborough and Great Coates survive on the main line, whilst North Kelsey, Moortown and Holton le Moor on the Lincoln branch are exquisite examples, each in a remote setting below the Wolds with only a few cottages and an inn for company. Brigg and Market Rasen justified larger facilities. Both had an overall roof and the main buildings were grand affairs in the Italianate style. Brigg featured a straightforward arcaded portico in contrast to

Market Rasen's entrance doorway with its intricate stonework. Kirton Lindsey was unlike any of the others – tall and somewhat stark. Extra–special treatment was given to Brocklesby, reflecting the influence of Lord Yarborough. It was a lively Jacobean composition with curly Dutch gables dominating all four elevations, and very tall chimneys. Habrough was rebuilt with staggered platforms and standard MS & L buildings when track alterations were carried out during 1883. Similarly, Barnetby underwent reconstruction in 1915 (this time with two large island platforms) at the culmination of the Wrawby Junction Brocklesby quadrupling. The detached office block, in particularly garish orange brick with a touch of 'Domestic Revival' ornamentation, represented the last phase of GC station architecture.

Early station closures were limited to Northorpe (1955) and Blyton (1959) on the main line, and Claxby & Usselby (1960) near Market Rasen. In 1961 Barnetby was served by 44 trains, a third of them still steam hauled. Fourteen were routed via Gainsborough, 13 via Market Rasen and 17 via Scunthorpe, with destinations including the now-

defunct Sheffield Victoria and Leeds Central. Pick up goods traffic virtually ceased in 1963–64 and on 1st November 1965 the Lincoln line lost its stopping service together with eight village stations. Paytrains and the associated withdrawal of station staff came on 29th June 1969. Barnetby had 47 trains in 1970 – 9 via Gainsborough, 16 via Market Rasen and 22 via Scunthorpe. By 1992 Sprinters had taken over and no less than 56 services paused at Barnetby – just six travelling along the old main line, 19 of them (including an HST to King's Cross and back) taking the Market Rasen route, and an impressive 31 passing through Scunthorpe. For the time being Wrawby Junction and Barnetby East signal boxes control a host of semaphore signals, although the route through the gap was reduced to two tracks in 1987. There were plans to reinstate one line during 1992. With its frequent service and remote location, Barnetby station has a certain affinity with long-gone Firsby in east Lincolnshire. But here the Station Inn did at least have illustrations of Great Central engines on the lounge walls!

Virtually all Cleethorpes holiday traffic passed through Barnetby and in the dying sunlight of a Sunday evening during June 1956 B1 No.61356 rushed through the station with a returning Doncaster excursion. The first coach is a brand new BR Standard Brake/2nd enjoying a running-in trip to the seaside before entering main line service. Photograph John Foreman.

On 1st July 1962 Leicester Midland 'Black 5' 4-6-0 No.45333 drew into Barnetby with a Hinckley – Cleethorpes special prior to taking water. The magnificent gantry was controlled by the now demolished Barnetby West signal box. Photograph John Foreman.

Reepham (Lincs) station – which gained the county suffix in 1923 to distinguish it from the ex-Great Eastern facilities in Norfolk – was typical of the delightful buildings on the Barnetby to Lincoln line. This particular example closed to goods traffic at the end of 1963 and passenger services ceased on 1st November 1965. It was business as usual, however, when the photograph was taken on 7th August 1959. Photograph H.B. Priestley.

Blast furnaces and buildings housing the gas engines which provided air for that blast formed a dramatic setting as class 02/2 2-8-0 No.63938 passed Frodingham Ironworks on 13th April 1954. Another 02/2 No.63937 stood in front of the Station Hotel and former Frodingham & Scunthorpe station, which succeeded the original Frodingham station in 1887 and was itself replaced by the present facilities during 1928. Photograph British Steel.

The Trent, Ancholme & Grimsby Railway was an immediate success and played a crucial role in the industrialisation of Scunthorpe, but working the heavy freight traffic has always been a challenge. Scunthorpe is on a plateau and the ascent from the Trent Valley involved a long 1 in 100 gradient incorporating the 85-arch Scotter Road viaduct, followed by 1 in 93 through a deep rock and shale cutting. Evening sunshine picked out class 04/1 2-8-0 No.63576 as it struggled up the bank in June 1957 with a full load of South Yorkshire coal. The 'Gunhouse Banker' – another 04 – was assisting at the back. Photograph John Foreman.

Chapter 31
Scunthorpe

Steelmaking at Anchor

The eastern approach consisted of a 1 in 96 rise to Santon. Grantham class 02/3 No.63948 and an 04/8 thundered through Appleby as they tackled the climb with a train of empty steel plate wagons from Annesley in April 1956. Photograph John Foreman.

North of Kirton the limestone uplands split into parallel ridges which culminate in prominent slopes overlooking the Humber near Alkborough and Winteringham. In the mid–1800s this area contained a scattering of farming villages, such as Burton–upon–Stather with its old houses of tobacco coloured brick, and Broughton with its fine Saxon church. Elsewhere, sandy heathland was given over to rabbit warrens and some local people earned a living by supplying furs to the London elite. At the time , Normanby Park, Appleby Hall, and the sleepy villages of Frodingham and Scunthorpe were little known outside these somewhat remote parts, but eventually their names became synonymous with the most spectacular of all heavy industries – iron and steel.

Rowland Winn of Appleby Hall was fully aware that iron had been mined locally in the distant past, so he set about re discovering this potential source of income. By 1859 the quest had been successful and his thoughts turned to selling ore to the ironmasters of Barnsley and Rotherham. Quarrying began in July 1860 and before long a primitive tramway was laid down to the Trent. But Winn became increasingly interested in building furnaces rather than just transporting ore and it was obvious that a proper railway would be needed.

The South Yorkshire Railway had reached Keadby on the far bank of the Trent in September 1859 and during 1861 Parliamentary approval was given for an extension eastwards through Frodingham to Barnetby in the form of the Trent, Ancholme & Grimsby Railway. This project was funded jointly by the SY, MS & L and Rowland

Winn, but difficulties with the Trent bridge delayed its opening for goods until 1st May 1866. Passenger services followed on 1st October. Meanwhile, the first furnaces had appeared. Trent, Frodingham and North Lincolnshire Ironworks were established close to the course of the new railway in 1864, 1865 and 1866 respectively. Local ore was proving a hazardous material to process and within a few months of being lit one of North Lincolnshire's furnaces exploded, showering molten iron far and wide and virtually wrecking the works. Despite such difficulties, the Frodingham – Scunthorpe area was on the brink of massive industrial change. The Lincolnshire, Redbourn and Appleby Ironworks were built between 1873 and 1876, and steel production began in 1890. Between 1850 and 1900 the population had risen from 1200 to over 10,000, as reflected by the scattering of industrial hamlets which had sprung up.

The North Lindsey Light Railway was opened from Scunthorpe to West Halton, Winteringham and Whitton on 3rd September 1906, 15th July 1907 and 1st December 1910 respectively to develop the area north of the growing town, and Normanby Park works was immediately built alongside it. By day the area had become a forest of smoking chimneys whilst at night the glow

from furnaces lit up the sky. Even the coat of arms granted to the newly formed Borough of Scunthorpe in 1936 featured a blast furnace and the mot to REFULGIT LABORES NOSTROS COELUM – The Heavens Reflect Our Labours. Two mighty blast furnaces were commissioned in 1939, followed by two more in 1954 when they were given the names *Mary, Bess, Anne and Victoria*. The four 'Queens' have dominated Scunthorpe's skyline ever since.

A major modernisation scheme known as the Anchor Project was announced shortly after the British Steel Corporation was formed in 1967. It envisaged a 50% increase in steel production and a mile-long mill for the production of billets. Railway modernisation took place concurrently, and Scunthorpe power box together with upgraded permanent way was brought into operation on 1st April 1973, in time for the completion of the BSC project. Inevitably there were railway casualties as well; closure of Winterton Mine in 1980 and Normanby Park works in 1981 drastically reduced traffic on the NLL railway which had lost its passenger services as long ago as 13th july 1925. These changes attracted little attention nationally, but the area really hit the headlines on 1st June 1974 when Flixborough Nypro works suffered a catastrophic explosion devastating surrounding property and even smashing dozens of windows in Scunthorpe, 3 miles away. It noise was clearly heard in East Hull all of 25 miles distant.

Scunthorpe is still a fascinating railway centre today. In 1992 virtually all raw material came in via Immingham Docks and this amounted to about 5 million tons a year. About 80 double headed trains a week brought South American, Australian and other foreign ore to the works, whilst other workings were required for the 2 million tons of Polish and Canadian coal. Billets for further processing were dispatched to Rotherham and Wolverhampton, a range of projects was sent to Cardiff, and part finished stee l was exchanged with Tees–side. Through freight included tanker trains to and from Immingham. Scunthorpe itself can hardly be described as picturesque, yet it is a clean, spacious place with lots of amenities and certainly does not deserve the jests meted out by generations of comedians. Even the impression of demonic energy once so characteristic of the town has disappeared with the installation of modern equipment and environmental improvements.

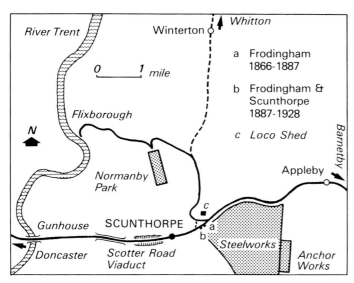

There was still a fair amount of freight traffic in the 1950s and this was worked by Ivatt 2MT 2-6-0s from Goole shed (25C). They looked very much at home on the line, as in the case of No.46407 heading north across Hatfield Waste Drain with the daily pick up goods. Photograph courtesy Neville Stead.

Reedness Junction was a desolate place at the end of a network of unsign-posted lanes leading to the edge of Thorne Waste and it owed its existence to the divergence of the Fockerby branch rather than a surfeit of potential customers. No.46407 posed against the plain station house and a North Eastern slotted post signal. Photograph courtesy Neville Stead.

Crowle viaduct was a particularly impressive structure for a light railway such as the Isle of Axholme Joint. The Ivatt 2MT was crossing the swinging span over the Stainforth & Keadby Canal and the end of the train is above the original South Yorkshire Railway route. Photograph Neville Stead Collection.

Chapter 32
Isle of Axholme

John Wesley

In 1742 John Wesley returned to his home village of Epworth to preach, but he was not allowed in the church and he addressed a captivated audience from his father's tombstone instead. Over the next fifty years the 'Father of Methodism' travelled tirelessly to share his faith, and Epworth has been a destination for pilgrims ever since. Otherwise this particular corner of Lincolnshire is little known. Much of it was waterlogged wasteland and was condemned by one observer as 'a mighty rude place.....the people being little better than heathen'. Hatfield Moors and Thorne Waste, to the north east of Doncaster, are still wild places – but the nearby Marshland lying in an angle between the Rivers Ouse and Trent was transformed into a rich agricultural area by patient drainage work. Epworth, Haxey, Belton and Crowle are long established farming villages, for they stand on a ridge known as the Isle of Axholme, rising clear of the expanse of peat moor, pools and swamp.

During the mid–1840s there was a distinct possibility that the main east coast railway would be built across the Isle of Axholme, but in reality it passed well to the west, and for many years the only track to penetrate the area was that between Doncaster and Scunthorpe. When a north–south line eventually materialised it was a purely local

Hatfield Moor, just over the border in Yorkshire, was one of the most remote termini in England and on this occasion provided Ivatt 2MT No.46436 with just two wagons. Photograph courtesy Neville Stead.

affair, yet managed to bring two mighty railway companies to Lincolnshire for the first time. However, neither the North Eastern nor the Lancashire & Yorkshire were really interested in the county – instead, both were eager to reach the expanding South Yorkshire coalfield and developments in the Isle of Axholme looked likely to provide a way through.

The initiative came from two modest concerns in search of agricultural traffic, encouraged by relaxed regulations permitted under the 1896 Light Railway Act. Authorisation for the Goole & Marshland Light Railway and the Isle of Axholme Light Railway in 1898 and 1899 respectively resulted in North Eastern goods trains reaching the Lincolnshire villages of Eastoft and Crowle by mid–1900. The NE and L & Y purchased the unfinished lines on 1st October 1902 and rechristened them the Isle of Axholme Joint Railway, but within twelve months plans for a direct line to the South Yorkshire collieries had been finalised, thus depriving the system of its strategic value. Passenger trains worked by L & Y 0–6–2 tanks began to run from Goole to Fockerby and Crowle on 10th August 1903, and through to Haxey Junction on 2nd January 1905.

Unlike many light railways, the Axholme system needed some substantial engineering works to carry its 27¾ miles of single track. The main line section from Marshland Junction to Crowle, together with the branches to Fockerby and Hatfield Moor (the latter opened for freight only on 22nd February 1909), were straightforward enough as they ran across almost perfectly level land. But the undulating Isle of Axholme itself presented more of a challenge, with virtually all of the formation from Belton to Haxey Junction made up of a succession of embankments and cuttings punctuated by bridges. The watercourses mid–way between Crowle and Belton were even more demanding. A viaduct comprising nine brick arches crossed Folly Drain and

South Level Engine Drain, whilst nearby another substantial structure took the rails across Hatfield Waste Drain and the River Torne. Just to the north stood Crowle viaduct, five brick arches, a girder span over the Doncaster – Scunthorpe line and a 104 ft. swinging section across the Stainforth & Keadby Canal.

By the early 1930s local buses had tempted most people away from the passenger trains, which in any case provided a very meagre service. So Sentinel steam railcar No. 44, introduced in 1930, ambled along from Haxey to Reedness Junction, visited Fockerby, and made its way to Goole for the last time on 15th July 1933. Nevertheless, special excursions continued to carry Methodists to Epworth and the goods yards remained busy. The Epworth–Haxey Junction section closed as an economy measure on 1st February 1956, facilities were withdrawn from the Hatfield Moor branch on 30th September 1963 and the six remaining goods yards finished on 5th April 1965. Until 1972 the track was retained as far as the site of the proposed Belton power station which never materialised, but otherwise the Isle of Axholme Joint passed into oblivion.

The NE and L & Y probably only expected a modest volume of passenger business and this was reflected in the somewhat basic stations – low unpaved platforms and a plain brick or timber waiting room was the norm. In marked contrast a large house was provided for the station master, and this normally incorporated booking facilities. Decorative work was kept to a minimum, although the later ones on the southern part of the 'main line' displayed a touch of half timbering at the gable ends, reflecting a weak concession to current architectural fashions. All but one of the dark red brick buildings survive, many of them a lengthy hike from the villages they once served.

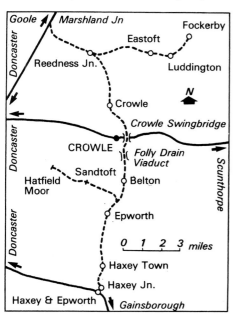

Map:

Goole / Marshland Jn — Fockerby
Eastoft
Doncaster
Reedness Jn.
Luddington
N
Crowle
Doncaster
Crowle Swingbridge
CROWLE
Folly Drain Viaduct
Sandtoft / Belton
Hatfield Moor
Scunthorpe
Doncaster
Epworth
0 1 2 3 miles
Haxey Town
Haxey Jn.
Haxey & Epworth / Gainsborough

89

In May 1956 Frodingham class 04/1 2-8-0 No.63696, fresh out of works, headed east across King George V Bridge, as an Austin Ruby bounced towards Keadby. The tall masts carried telegraph wires to the Gunness side of the Trent where the 'Gunhouse Banker' was attached to help the heavy coal train up to Scunthorpe. Traffic on the A18 has grown enormously since 1956 resulting in new bracing spans to increase headroom on the road part of the bridge and a separate pedestrian way outside the main girders. Photograph John Foreman.

Frodingham class 04/7 2-8-0 No.63884 arriving at Keadby Canal Junction with a regular trip working of empty mineral wagons from Scunthorpe one day in summer 1962. The engine then pushed them into Keadby Down Sidings which occupied the western approach to the original Trent swingbridge. Prominent in this view is the very rare sliding bridge where the railway crosses the Keadby Canal. It is equipped with wheels and rolls back behind the signal box on a set of rails at right angles to the waterway. Direct current drive motors are activated by an ancient tramcar-type controller at the far side of the box. The bridge regularly opens two or three times a day for pleasure boats and is operated in the same way, albeit under the control of Doncaster power box. Photograph John Foreman.

Chapter 33

Crossing the Trent

Gainsborough Bridge

Newark is nearly 50 miles from the mouth of the Trent, but for centuries its medieval bridge was the lowest point where a crossing could be made other than by boat. One such ferry was at Gainsborough. In 1760 it capsized with the loss of six lives when a man on horseback leaped aboard, and this incident prompted the construction of a replacement bridge, completed thirty years later. Then in 1824 a toll bridge was erected at Dunham mid-way between Newark and Gainsborough. Despite these developments the Trent was still a hindrance to trade, yet it was also a major artery itself. Items such as Staffordshire pottery and Derbyshire iron were brought downstream and transferred from river craft to sea–going boats at Gainsborough, where the wharves and riverside warehouses teemed with activity. The town even had a thriving ship-building industry which was at its height when the Gainsborough – Hull paddle steamer *John Bull* was launched in 1815. The completion of the Manchester, Sheffield & Lincolnshire Railway main line 34 years later was a serious blow to activity on the river, although by then silting was a problem and traffic had already begun to decline.

Spanning the Trent at Gainsborough was a major achievement for the MS & L. Maintenance of a clearway for navigation and the establishment of firm footings for the piers were challenging enough tasks, but placing the two 154 ft. main girders into position caused untold anxiety. The bridge opened on 16th April 1849. A week earlier services began over the Great Northern line from Lincoln. Initially trains reversed into Gainsborough station but with the completion of the MS & L westwards, through workings to Doncaster commenced and the GN's own facilities at Lea Road followed. From 7th August 1850 this service was able to use the shorter Leverton route which incorporated a big wrought iron bridge over the Trent at Torksey. A further diversion came on 15th July 1867 when the direct GN line to Doncaster opened. By this time another bridge had been completed at Keadby, 15 miles downstream. It opened on 1st May 1866 to link the South Yorkshire Railway with Scunthorpe's infant iron industry and featured a 160 ft. swinging span in its 484 ft. deck. Numerous boat accidents had brought adverse publicity during its construction, and the port of Gainsborough showed hostility throughout. Finally, the Barlborough – Lincoln section of the hopelessly over–ambitious Lancashire, Derbyshire & East Coast Railway opened for goods on 16th November 1896 crossing the Trent at Fledborough on four 110 ft. steel spans approached by 59 brick arches. Only a third of this massive 170 mile line from Warrington to Sutton on Sea materialised and the proposed docks on the east coast were never started. Essentially it became an extravagant eastern outlet for the Derbyshire coalfield, which benefitted the Great Eastern Railway more than most.

In 1910 a fifth rail crossing of the lower Trent was proposed by the Trent Railway & Bridge Company, which was really a Lancashire & Yorkshire Railway plot to gain a share of the abundant South Humberside traffic. It envisaged a combined rail and road viaduct east of Fockerby, but the scheme was successfully quashed by the Great Central. Instead, the GC itself embarked on an ambitious replacement for the ailing Keadby swingbridge. Improved clearance for shipping and the inclusion of a roadway were considerations. A design patented by the Scherzer Rolling Lift Bridge Company of the USA was chosen, preparatory work began in 1912, and after almost a £¼ million had been spent on the mighty structure and its associated deviation line the King George V bridge opened on 21st May 1916.

Four granite piers supported the girders across the Trent and two of them were less than 40 ft. apart, for they bore the full 3,000 ton weight of the lift span and its concrete filled counterbalance when the bridge was raised. Petrol engines housed under the eastern approach span generated electricity for the lift motors.

Railways made a varied architectural contribution to the Trent valley. Saxilby station on the GN line west of Lincoln was a confused composition dominated by gables and chimneys which had an affinity with those at Lincoln Central, whilst buildings on the Gainsborough – Doncaster line, also in yellow brick, heralded GN standardisation. The South Yorkshire Railway put up basic red brick affairs which would have been more at home in the back streets of Barnsley, and they varied from a rambling two storey house at Keadby to the tiny hut at Godnow Bridge. Clifton was typical of the LD & EC's vaguely Jacobean style, and Althorpe on the Keadby bridge deviation displayed fashionable mock-Tudor half timbering. The 'tour de force' was undoubtedly Gainsborough Central. It had the usual MS & L overall roof, but the frontage was particularly impressive. A grand arcaded portico featuring Ionic columns was flanked by long single storey wings culminating in end blocks matching the entrance. In later years a siding was laid immediately in front of the facade and a lean–to shed covering the associated subway completely ruined its appearance.

Early passenger closures included the old SY terminus at Keadby in 1874 and remote Godnow Bridge, which lost its two trains a week in 1917. Complete service withdrawals have been limited to those over the LD & EC, on 19th September 1955 and via Torksey on 2nd November 1959. But the erstwhile MS & L main line between Gainsborough and Barnetby has recently been under threat and is already largely single track. The mouldering edifice at Gainsborough Central has been replaced by a bus shelter and for several years these have only been about half a dozen trains a day. Facilities and services at Lea Road are much better, with 35 departures on weekdays in 1992. Even the settings of the two stations seem to sympathise with their respective fortunes. Lea Road is surrounded by trees whilst Central hides behind Marshall's massive Britannia engineering works, now largely disused. Manufacturing industry developed in Gainsborough following the decline in river trade, but was accompanied by some of the worst slum housing in Lincolnshire. Further north, King George V bridge ceased lifting in 1958 and the frustrating occasions when it refused to close properly were no more. It is now the limit of navigation for large ships, although European freighters regularly visit nearby Keadby and Gunness wharves. Althorpe's attractive station buildings have gone, apart from the sad skeleton of a waiting shelter, but the railway is still very busy and it is worth spending some time on the footbridge. Approaching trains can been seen as far away as Crowle and Scunthorpe cutting, and heavy eastbound freights preparing to tackle Gunness bank are particularly impressive. The nearby Ironstone Wharf pub, recalling Rowland Winn's enterprise, offers hospitality away from the chilly Trent breeze and is as good a place as any to contemplate the fascinating railway system which once served Lincolnshire.

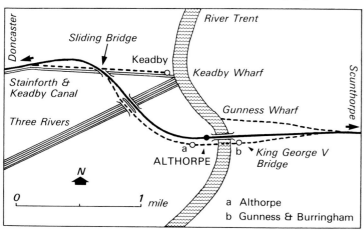

Doncaster
River Trent
Sliding Bridge
Keadby
Keadby Wharf
Scunthorpe
Stainforth & Keadby Canal
Three Rivers
Gunness Wharf
a   b King George V Bridge
ALTHORPE
N
0   1 mile
a Althorpe
b Gunness & Burringham

An elegant piece of Great Northern design deep in the Fens during 1970.

ACKNOWLEDGEMENTS

The overall look at Lincolnshire's railways relied heavily on help in the form of illustrations, information or both from a number of people specialising in particular areas of the country. In this respect I am indebted to John Foreman, John Clay, Les Perrin, R.C.Riley, John Bosner, H.B.Priestley, John Wilson, Alf Ludlarn, Barry Hilton, Neville Stead, David Swale, John Edgington, Graham Wise, Mick Black, A.G.W. Garraway, Horace Gamble, Archie Osborne and Harry Wilkinson. Special thanks to Roger Hockney for the help with the Grimsby area and proof reading, Ray Webster for several unusual illustrations and a critical appraisal of the text, and Vic Forster for his straightforward comments and persuading Jack Cupit to let me use some of his superb photographs. Finally a personal thankyou to Irwell Press for accepting an already completed work and remodelling it in their own style.

Looking west from Midville along the route of the New Line in 1988.